"In a sideways-glancing, elbow-jamming, s[...] *parison Girl* supplies an upside-down appr[...] Shannon Popkin exposes the crippling effe[...] [...] our forward motion in the kingdom, yet she also demonstrates how healthy comparison can inspire us to rise up and walk free. Discover how to exchange feelings of superiority for a lifestyle of service and feelings of inferiority for a lifetime of belonging."

Katie M. Reid, author of *Made Like Martha* and cohost of *The Martha & Mary Show* podcast

"If you struggle with measuring up, if you're worried about what people think, if you dread someone seeing you in a less than ideal situation, then you're human. We all struggle with comparing ourselves to others. That means we all need Shannon's honest and wise words on the pages of this book. I know I did, and I'm betting you do too!"

Jill Savage, author of *No More Perfect Moms*

"In *Comparison Girl*, Shannon combines Jesus's teachings with brilliant spiritual insights and powerful tools like the 'Disgust Factor Challenge' that invite you to leave comparison behind in favor of freedom in Christ. If you want to love people more, let go of beating yourself up, and shake off our culture's me-first mindset, then grab *Comparison Girl* and gather some friends so you can share this experience together."

Barb Roose, speaker and author of *Surrendered* and *Winning the Worry Battle*

"What you're holding in your hands isn't a much-needed book; it's a desperately needed battle plan! With a humble pen and a bold honesty, Shannon invites us to look closely at our subtle 'comparison game' and recognize the truth behind it: comparison is not just a harmless habit but an all-out attack on the life we've been created to live. Using the very words of Jesus, Shannon shows us how to trade the exhaustion of measure-up comparison for the exhilaration of me-free living. If you're tired of letting the enemy use comparison to confiscate your joy, steal your significance, and destroy your relationships, this book will equip you to fight back!"

Alicia Bruxvoort, speaker and writer with Proverbs 31 Ministries

"Shannon Popkin has masterfully written another must-read to speak to the struggles of our soul. Like a dear friend she sits with us and soothes us with the truth of how purposefully we were created, how intentionally we have been gifted, and how infinitely we are loved. Inviting us to listen to the tender truths of God and silence the enemy's lies, Shannon shows us how to live freely in a culture of continual comparison. For every woman who wonders if she is truly enough—here is your answer."

Erica Wiggenhorn, author of *Unexplainable Jesus*

"*Comparison Girl* is a needed resource for today's women. I love how Shannon takes us through comparison in Scripture, acknowledging how normal it is for us to compare but also providing biblical principles for taking our eyes off of others and directing them to Jesus Christ."

Brenda Yoder, LMHC, speaker and author of *Fledge*

"Shannon Popkin helps us take a fresh and challenging look at the everyday mindsets we wrestle with. Showing us God's higher ways straight from the life of Jesus, she calls us from our me-focused thinking to His kingdom-focused purposes. After this study and with the power of the Holy Spirit, I won't allow those thoughts to stay around any longer."

Lynn Cowell, author of *Make Your Move*

"Comparison is a sneaky issue that can work its way into almost any situation. But is all comparison bad? Through her in-depth study of the Scriptures, Shannon Popkin reveals two sides to this prevalent issue: negative, sinful comparison and positive, biblical comparison. This book convicted me of the sinful tendencies hidden in my heart and encouraged me to view myself and others through the eyes of Christ."

Kate Motaung, author of *A Place to Land*

"I am a Comparison Girl. I never wanted to play into the enemy's plan for dismantling my contentment and peace, and I suspect you don't want to either. So it's high time we cast aside our measuring mentality and adopt a new way. Shannon Popkin expertly walks us through the markers and mistakes of this measure-up world and gently points us to a better way. With humor and brutal honesty, Shannon fights for her readers' hearts with biblical wisdom, humility, and truth."

Lee Nienhuis, author and host of the *Moms in Prayer* podcast

Comparison Girl

Lessons *from* Jesus *on* Me-Free Living
in a Measure-Up World

SHANNON POPKIN

KREGEL
PUBLICATIONS

To my three kids: Lindsay, Cole, and Cade.
May you always find confidence, freedom, and joy in living by the
spout, not the lines.

Contents

Acknowledgments

KEN, THANKS FOR encouraging me to pour out every last drop required to write this book. My writing would not be possible without your love and support. I'm so grateful to have you by my side, making me laugh, helping me stay focused on our kingdom goals, and sharing the treasure of life. You are such a gift to me.

Lindsay, your sweet faithfulness to Jesus and trust in him as a college student gives me more joy than I could ever express. Cole, I am celebrating with you over all God has done, and I am so incredibly proud of you. Cade, watching you serve others with your music, your words, and your humor gives me such deep joy. Sometimes one of you leans over to ask me if those are tears in my eyes and why on earth I am crying. More often than not, here's why: Watching the three of you explore life and set out on the adventure of pouring out your gifts into the world as worship before God creates such stirring joy. Tears are all I have to express it.

Mom and Dad, thanks for being 6 a.m. workers in the vineyard (Matt. 20) who taught me the joy and honor of serving Jesus. Your love for the Lord was the foundation for mine. Thanks for loving our kids, investing in all of us, and serving up "feast night" week after week. I'm so grateful for both of you.

Rachel Norton, Jamie Brauns, Jackie VanDyke, and Kristi Huseby—you are each true friends who inspire me to follow Jesus with sweet abandon. Thanks for investing in me, sharing life, and always reminding me of what's true.

The Prayeriors—this book wouldn't be possible without your prayers. Thank you for your commitment to serve alongside me in this way. Special thanks to Ruth, Aunt Jo, Pearl, Karen, and Bonnie for all the notes of encouragement, texts, and verses. Knowing you pray encourages me more than you know.

Pearl Allard and Erika VanHaitsma, you are the best assistants one could ask for! Thank you for supporting me with such excellence and joy. And a special thanks to Johanna Froese (and Pearl's hand!) for the cover image on this book.

Vivian Mabuni, Kate Motaung, Lee Nienhuis, Katie Reid, and Brenda Yoder—thanks for your partnership as we minister with words. Your collective wisdom has been such a gift. Grinklings—thank you for praying for me, sharing your input, and offering encouragement.

Thanks to the team at Kregel for investing in me and going the extra mile on this project! Janyre and Sarah—you both take the "i" out of editor in a big way. Thanks to Catherine, Steve, Katherine, Joel, and the many other hands rowing in the same direction. May the Lord be pleased with our work. Thanks also to Paul Genzink for his amazing videographer work. You turned spoken ideas and a room full of friends into a powerful Bible study resource.

And to the Lord Jesus, who made himself small and poured himself out so that he could snatch me back from wandering into destruction, *thank you*. I have loved learning the sound of your voice as I've studied the pages of your Word. Thank you for the privilege of sharing these thoughts about you with my friends.

Introduction

The Makings of a Comparison Girl

I'VE HEARD THAT your earliest memory says something about what's important to you. Mine took place at church when I was about four years old. We were in the balcony area, and I had been allowed to sit all by myself one row ahead of my parents and off to the side. I remember feeling oh so grown-up as I held my hymnbook high and sang along proudly. But then came an interruption.

I was startled by a lady behind me who leaned down to help turn my hymnbook (which *she* apparently thought was upside down) right side up. As she placed it back in my hands, I scowled. The woman and her friends were looking down at me with sweet yet patronizing smiles, and I didn't like it. Not one bit.

I whipped myself forward with my head held high and flipped my hymnbook back the other way. This is how I *liked* holding my hymnbook, thank you very much. So there.

From my earliest years, I have loathed those moments when my shortcomings become painfully obvious. I despise being exposed or looked down upon. I prefer for the whole world to see me as a vision of sparkly perfection, as someone who has absolutely no flaws at all. Even when my deficiency is to be expected (like not being able to read at age four), my heart is bent on perfectionism, independence, and pride.

As you can imagine, this tendency has not led to great freedom and joy. Instead it's led to a great fear of what people think and what they might say, a great drive to prove myself and measure up, and a great dread of being found lacking.

These fears, drives, and dreads are the makings of a Comparison Girl.

LESS THAN

Darla was one of my dearest friends in college. She and I had so much fun together, laughing wherever we went. But there was one category in which I felt vastly inferior to Darla: dating.

Darla had one boyfriend after another. If she tossed one guy back out to sea, not a week would go by before she was reeling in some new "catch." I, on the other hand, had far less dating experience. Once in a while I was asked on a date, and occasionally a short-lived relationship would blossom. But where Darla's dating calendar had only a few open spots, mine had only a few filled.

We never discussed this. I never said to Darla, "Why do more guys like you than me?" But I wondered. Was she prettier than me? Was she more fun to talk to? Was her personality more magnetic?

I didn't let these nagging questions wiggle their way to the surface much. I loved my friend, and I didn't want to be jealous of her, so I kept my comparing private. I *certainly* wouldn't have chosen for my dating inadequacies (especially in comparison to Darla) to be put on public display! But that's exactly what happened.

Darla and I were with a group of students at someone's apartment one day when somebody decided it would be fun to play a How Well Do You Know Your Date game. To play, several of the boyfriends in the group went into the kitchen to write down answers to a list of questions while their girlfriends stayed back in the living room. When the guys came out, if the girls' answers to the same questions matched what their boyfriends had said, they would earn points.

There weren't enough couples, so Darla and I agreed to play as roommates. She went into the kitchen and I stayed behind, grinning when little Darla filed out with the broad-shouldered boyfriends, each of them carrying a stack of answers on notecards.

I only remember one question from that game—the one that made my heart sink. The question was "How often do you go out on dates?" Here were my options:

A. At least once a week
B. Once every other week
C. Once a month
D. Less than once a month

How often did I go out on dates? Hardly ever! D was the obvious answer. But I wasn't about to disclose *that*—not in a room full of guys I'd *like* to date! I cringed at being known as "the girl who never gets asked out."

I only had a few seconds to prepare my answer, and the rationalization that went zipping around in my brain went something like this: "Okay, in the past year I've dated one, two . . . three guys, I think. And each time, I had about . . . um . . . maybe four or five dates? That's fifteen dates. About. We'll round up to fifteen. So if you divide fifteen by twelve, that's more than one per month. On average. So it's safe to say that I go out on dates more than once a month . . ."

"B," I answered confidently. "Every other week."

Darla immediately looked puzzled. It was her turn to flip over the piece of paper in her hands and reveal her answer, but she didn't. She just stood there in that row of boyfriends, looking at me with a questioning gaze.

Suddenly, my heart filled with dread. Thinking only of the impression I would make on the others, I hadn't factored in the fact that Darla was not privy to my secret game of multiplication-rationalization. With the soft tone you might use to gently correct a lying child, she said, "Shan . . ." It was clear that our answers did not match. It was also clear that I was about to be pegged as "the girl who never gets asked out but pretends she does." I was mortified.

The others waited in silence, looking back and forth between Darla and me as our eyes remained locked. I could tell by her pleading expression that she wanted me to change my answer, but that would be even more mortifying! To publicly label myself "the girl who never gets asked out but pretends—then confesses" was just too embarrassing. I couldn't do it.

After delaying as long as she could, Darla raised her truth-revealing card.

"D. Less than once a month."

It was a sickening moment for me. An entire group of my peers had witnessed my obvious attempt at inflating my dating history, then watched it shrivel back down to its actual size.

For many, many years, I never spoke of that event. Not even with Darla. It wasn't until I was recounting college stories for my daughter (who attends the same university I did) that I was able to finally share—and laugh about—my dating life exposé experience. My daughter giggled, wide-eyed, and said, "Oh, Mom, that's so *awful!*"

I agree. It was!

Despised Inadequacy

Has there ever been some truth about yourself that you tried to keep hidden? Do you have any memories from decades past that are frozen in shame, too difficult to tell another soul? Have you ever stretched the truth like a rubber band to make yourself look better only to have it snap back in your face?

There is something in us that despises our own inadequacy. We loathe being thought of as "less than." We long to be accepted and admired. Not overlooked or excluded. We want to measure up! And so we fall into the habit of glancing sideways to measure ourselves against others.

Have you seen those laser tape measures that flash a little red beam, then give instantaneous measurements? When I was a teen and young adult, my mind was like a laser tape measure that never shut off. Wherever I went, I was taking measurements and wondering how I compared. I was consumed with thoughts like:

What does he think of me?
How do I look right now?
Am I as pretty as she is?
Did that sound dumb?

I didn't talk openly about my insecurities. I'm sure many of my peers thought I was confident and strong, but in the privacy of my heart, I was constantly measuring myself against others. I craved knowing what people thought. How *they* measured me. How I ranked in comparison with others.

When someone gave me a compliment, I treated it like pure gold. I would carefully tuck each one into little file cabinets in my mind, returning to my files often to assure myself that I wasn't completely lacking.

I also intuitively learned to use comparison to douse my insecurity with pride. I would purposely look for a girl who *didn't* measure up to me in some way. Maybe she wasn't as smart or well-liked. Or she wasn't quite as pretty. I would console myself, thinking, *At least I'm better than her.* I told myself I was practicing gratitude, but really I was fostering pride.

THE MOST

One day when I was a young teacher, my principal pulled me aside and said, "Shannon, I want you to know, out of all the teachers in the building, we've received the most parent requests for *you*. Keep up the good work!" My heart just about exploded with pride.

I was requested! I was *more* requested than the others! I modestly kept this information to myself, but in the months to come, whenever I made a mistake or someone challenged my work, I would comfort myself with the memory of my principal's compliment. I would recall his exact words and use them to push away my rising self-doubt. Then months turned into years.

I'm ashamed to think about how many times I reviewed those words. Years later, when those parents were as likely to remember which parking space they chose on the first day of school as they were to remember which teacher they requested for their child, I was still dragging around the tattered memory of this expired compliment, like Linus with his security blanket. *You were the most requested that year,* I would tell myself. *The most!*

It's embarrassing to share that with you. It kind of turns my stomach.

And it's even harder to admit that comparison still plagues me today. I still sometimes worry more about what people think than what God thinks. And I still intuitively want to douse my insecurity with nice things people have said to me. As soon as this book comes out, I'm sure I'll be tempted to obsess over its reviews and Amazon rankings.

Social media doesn't help me with this, by the way. I have such compassion for today's kids who grow up with live data that they can use to measure themselves against others. They don't have to wonder what people think; Instagram and Snapchat offer proof.

I have compassion for us grown-ups too. We've moved beyond comparing ourselves with other girls sitting in our classroom at school. Now we have social media to blow back the curtains on a million women at once, allowing us to gather tangible evidence on how we rank. Who takes more and better vacations than we do. Who spends more time on crafts and outings with their kids. Whose house is tidier and more updated than ours. Whose high schooler poses for selfies with Mom while mine requires a football field's length between us at social events.

Comparison, I've learned, is like a drug. The more we do it, the more we want to. It becomes a compulsion to check how we're measuring up. With our phones always at hand, it's nearly impossible for us to make it through even one afternoon without checking on our tallied clicks, likes, and comments.

Comparison isn't something we keep compartmentalized either. It seeps into every part of our lives and follows us into every stage. We compare from the time we're young moms until the time we're grandmas, from the time we're new employees until we're retirees, from the time we're new brides until we're fiftieth-anniversary celebrators. We simply can't stop doing this thing that robs us of our joy, drains our sense of significance, and holds us back. We can't stop playing the "comparison game."

BUT IS IT A GAME?

It's ironic that we call comparison a game, because I'm pretty sure Satan thinks of comparison as a war strategy that he uses against us. Here's what makes me say that. Comparison has two outcomes. Sometimes we compare and consider ourselves superior, which leads to:

- pride
- self-focus
- obsessive goal-setting
- perfectionism
- judgmental criticism
- inflated arrogance
- obsession with performance

Other times we compare and consider ourselves inferior, which leads to:

- humiliation
- self-consciousness
- obsessive fears
- resignation
- insecurity
- worthlessness
- shame
- self-loathing
- jealousy

I don't want to be characterized by any of these, and I'm guessing you feel the same. These are the ugly vices we'd like to be free of. They hold us captive, often for decades, which is exactly what Satan wants. Measure-up comparison isn't a game; it's an attack. And if we're ever going to escape, we've got to recognize our misconceptions and the enemy prompting us to believe them.

The next time you hear a voice saying, "Look at that woman. She's so much thinner than you," please note that this is never Jesus speaking, always your enemy. And when you hear a voice saying, "Look at her. She obviously doesn't know what's in style," remember that this is never Jesus speaking, always your enemy.

KING JESUS

Perhaps you've heard the famous quote attributed to President Theodore Roosevelt, "Comparison is the thief of joy." And if you're like me, you expect Scripture to back that up. But it doesn't. In fact, I often hear Jesus inviting us to compare. Do you find that hard to believe?

When Jesus came, walking in sandals on dusty roads and sharing our meals, stories, and pain, he encountered Comparison Girls who were plagued with just as much jealousy, arrogance, condescension, and shame as we are. Yet Jesus didn't teach them to renounce all comparison. Instead, many of his lessons included comparisons to make his point. Think of the stories Jesus told of the Good Samaritan, the Pharisee and the tax collector, and the wise and foolish builders.

Jesus also compared people in real life. Like when a widow donated two practically worthless copper coins, and Jesus said she gave more than the others. Or when Martha was complaining that her sister wasn't helping in the kitchen, and Jesus said Mary had chosen what was better. Jesus used comparison words and comparison stories all the time, teaching a new upside-down way of seeing things.

In the world, there is a particular way that things stack up. There's a system in place, which works like this. If you want to be somebody in the eyes of the world, you have to outdo somebody else. If you want to be honored, you have to get ahead. If you want to be important, you have to prove that you have more and are more. In short, you have to measure up. And from the way we all scramble to try to do so, it seems obvious we've gotten the memo. Yet here's what we forget.

This measure-up world and its ruler, Satan, are the two great enemies of God. It is out of hostility toward God that these enemies entice me to live by the world's rules and play its games. And then there's one more enemy: me. Because as the world and the devil call out, "Come play the comparison game," here's my reality: I want to play! I want to be jealous. I want to push ahead. I want to pout when somebody else gets ahead. Yet when I cave in to my sinful desire to measure up, I participate in a world system led by an evil ruler who wants to destroy me.

One day very soon, Jesus will return to set up his kingdom, and on that day the tables will turn. Everything in the world will be realigned under King Jesus. Many who are overlooked, undervalued, or considered "lasts" in this life will be the great ones in the life to come.

Jesus invites you and me to live now the way we'll wish we had then—rejecting our measure-up cravings and pursuing the rewards of his kingdom instead of the fading rewards of the world. To be sure, we won't get total relief from the comparison battle until the day Satan is banished and all is made new. But today, when I choose to live by Jesus's kingdom values, it's like stepping away from the world's measure-up smog to breathe in the clean air of the kingdom.

RED-LETTER COMPARISONS

Okay, but how do I make the switch? How do I deny my inner Comparison Girl and leave my measure-up ways behind? How do I turn to follow Jesus instead? Here's how: I learn to listen to the voice of Jesus. I listen long enough and intently enough that I begin to know what Jesus sounds like. So much so that when I hear some message like, "You're worthless" or start to think, "You're better than her," I know enough to say, "Uh . . . that's not something Jesus would say." The more I listen to Jesus, the more I think about what I'm thinking. Rather than blindly entertaining sinful, me-focused ideas, I start to recognize the enemy's hiss in my own thoughts.

Jesus said that his sheep follow him for they know his voice (John 10:4), and thankfully his voice is recorded on the pages of our Bibles. As we lean in to listen, we'll repeatedly hear Jesus talking about his kingdom. He was always using pithy, upside-down statements to describe how his kingdom stands in contrast to the world. I think he wanted these statements to stick in people's minds and help reshape the way they looked at themselves, others, and the world. I think he wants the same for Comparison Girls today. That's why I arranged this study around what I call the "red-letter comparisons" of Jesus.

I first encountered the red-letter comparisons of Jesus back when I spent my days wiping little noses and bottoms and folding miniature pairs of jeans—and comparing myself with women whose daily agendas seemed far more important and worthy. In my validation-craving frustration, I remember paging through my Bible looking for the red-letter verses, which I knew marked the very words of Jesus. I longed to hear directly from my Lord and gain his perspective on my life rather than being taunted by the less-than messages of my enemy. This exercise did not disappoint.

As I sat in my toy-strewn living room, wearing no makeup and a spit-up-stained sweatshirt, the red-letter comparisons of Jesus came alive. Here's what I heard Jesus saying.

The greatest among us is she who serves.

She who exalts herself will be humbled, and she who humbles herself will be exalted.

She who is first will be last. She who is last will be first.

I was intrigued. It settled my heart to know that greatness wasn't tied to a paycheck or title. If it was true that I could become one of the "kingdom greats" simply by stooping down to serve, my living room provided ample opportunity.

I pulled out a notebook and began listing out Jesus's upside-down teachings. As I studied, I noticed that Jesus wasn't just dropping in his red-letter comparisons randomly; he was purposefully weaving them into stories and conversations with people who—like me—were comparing.

Jesus was responding in real time to real people who were:

- Comparing their sin with others' sin
- Comparing their wealth and possessions
- Comparing their appearances
- Comparing their work for God
- Comparing their status

As I listened in on these interactions between Jesus and comparison-prone people from centuries past, it was like finding myself in the Bible. I saw myself in the disciples who craved recognition. I saw myself in the Pharisees, wearing flashy clothes to be seen. I saw myself in the tax collector who felt ashamed because of his sin. And I saw myself in the man who didn't want to give away his money and become average. In each instance, there was much for me to learn from Jesus about his upside-down kingdom.

Although my kids have outgrown those miniature jeans I used to fold, the teachings of Jesus have continued to steady me. Today, my living room is tidy, and titles and paychecks are the norm, but I'm still prone to Comparison Girl measuring. More than ever, I need to guard myself from my invasive enemy by listening to the voice of my shepherd. Returning regularly to the red-letter comparisons of Jesus is like having that hymnbook in my four-year-old hands put right. I can't say that it's a comfortable or easy exercise; it's often quite humbling. But reorienting myself to Jesus's perspective is what settles my heart and restores my confidence and joy.

LIVING ME-FREE

If you struggle with measure-up comparison as I do, I invite you to join me for a six-week study of Jesus's red-letter comparisons and the stories and conversations they are tucked into. I suggest keeping a red pen handy so you can mark your book and your Bible when you come across the red-letter comparisons of Jesus. You'll be surprised at how many times they appear, and you'll be amazed at the way these statements—with red-ink intensity—can realign your thinking and help you see yourself and others from a kingdom perspective.

As we study together, you'll notice one key theme. The measure-up comparison that traps me is entirely me-focused. When I enter a room of people, I might be glancing around at others, but my focus always boomerangs back to me. I project and posture. I shrink and avoid. No matter what direction I turn, I'm thinking about me and obsessing over how I measure up—which is utterly exhausting. But if I enter a room full of people with the me-*free* mindset of Jesus, I'm able to simply focus on the other people in the room. Of course I'll still notice the ways I'm different, but my differences don't add to or detract from my value; they offer me unique ways to serve. Lifting up God and others with what I have and who I am gives me a place to belong—which isn't exhausting; it's exhilarating.

This me-free living is what guards against me-first comparison. When I put someone else ahead of me, I naturally stop trying to get ahead of her. And when I lift her up, I simultaneously stop looking down on her. And when I bend down to serve her, I forget to measure myself against her.

Me-free comparison looks at someone else and says, "What do I uniquely have to offer this person?" Or, "In what way has God gifted her to help me grow?" When I celebrate my own differentness and refuse to be threatened by the differentness I see in somebody else, it turns the tables on my entire life. When I'm not tethered to measure-up fear or get-ahead pride, I can embrace relationships, share my gifts, and enjoy God in ways that were never before possible. I can live me-free! Which means living

- free from self-doubt;
- free from jealousy and envy;
- free from the sting of not measuring up;
- free from self-centeredness and self-focus;
- free from endless striving to outdo others or get ahead;
- free to be the unique individual God designed me to be;
- free to encourage and cheer others on; and
- free to pour myself out and serve with joy.

Of course, all this is exactly what Satan *doesn't* want. He knows that participating in a community of people who are all serving each other and glorifying God is what protects us from bondage—while comparison keeps us stumbling back into it. So Satan will keep tempting us into me-first comparison. And Jesus will keep inviting us to live me-free. Do you long for the freedoms on that list the way I do? I'm so excited to experience me-free living with you as we study Jesus's red-letter comparisons and learn to do life like he did.

ABOUT THE STUDY

I hope you'll consider doing this study with a friend or in a group. If you'd like to have me be part of your group time with additional teaching on the topic of comparison, please check out my *Comparison Girl* teaching videos (sold separately).

I've divided the chapters into lessons—some chapters have more lessons than others—each beginning with a correlating Bible passage. Please don't skip these Bible readings; I wouldn't want you to miss out on hearing from Jesus directly. Though I've read these stories dozens of times, Jesus's upside-down perspective becomes a little sharper each time I reread. I'm eager for you to experience this as well.

You'll notice that each lesson concludes with a meditation that encapsulates the lesson's truth, plus some application and Bible study questions to make your study personal. I hope you'll use a notebook or the companion journal we've put together for you to record your responses and action plans. You can find the journal and other printable resources, including a leader's discussion guide, at ComparisonGirl .com.

Friend, let's put a stop to these comparison attacks that our enemy has been using against us for far too long. Instead of measuring ourselves against each other, let's exalt God and serve one another. Instead of being plagued by measure-up, get-ahead comparison, let's pour our lives out and be free.

Grab your journal and record some "Comparison Girl starting point" thoughts:

≈ Which of the motivators below are you most driven by?
- A desire to prove yourself and measure up
- A fear of what people think and what they'll say
- A dread of being found lacking

≈ Which of my stories can you best relate to, and why?
- The flipped hymnbook: wanting to be seen as someone with no flaws
- The dating life exposé: the temptation to inflate the truth about yourself
- The teacher request: dousing your insecurities with pride

≈ Think back over your past season of life. How has comparing yourself with others robbed you of your joy, drained your sense of significance, or held you back?

≈ Which of these would you most like to be free of?
  • Self-doubt
  • Jealousy and envy
  • Self-focus and the sting of not measuring up
  • Endless striving to outdo or get ahead

≈ Do you struggle more with feelings of inferiority or superiority? What would those who love you say? Perhaps you could ask someone, if you wish.

≈ What do you think God wants to transform most about the way you see yourself and others through this study?

Chapter One

From Measuring Up to Pouring Out

MY FRIEND ALISON had the horrific experience of watching her house go up in flames while she and her family watched from the front lawn. As they crossed the dark street—barefoot and pajama clad—to put some distance between themselves and the fire, a man pulled his car over to the side of the road. "Is that your house?" he asked.

Later, they learned he was the serial arsonist who had *set* the fire.

Apparently this isn't as unusual as it might sound. Criminologists have found that it's common for serial arsonists to return to the blaze they've just set and gaze upon the scene with a sense of power and importance.[1]

This, I believe, is how Satan looks at us as the destructive flames of comparison lick at our lives.

He's content to remain in the shadows, gazing with gratification as we pull away from each other in jealousy or pride. But in this chapter, I'd like to pull back the shadowy curtain and shine a spotlight on the enemy who's been setting his fires and driving us apart for far too long with his green-eyed wisdom.

Let's collapse these comparison walls between us and come together in me-free humility—lifting high our king Jesus and giving each other a place to belong.

Lesson 1: The Lines or the Spout
Read James 3:13–18 and John 10:1–11

IN SIXTH GRADE, I was a giggly, imaginative, carefree girl with glasses and freckles. My best friend, Kathy, and I amused ourselves by passing tiny notes—tucked into my pencil sharpener—which contained lots of code words in case we ever got caught. We had lots of sleepovers, giggling into the night over the silly fill-in-the-blank stories we made up.

Then everything changed at sixth grade camp. Kath was in a different cabin, and I was with some girls who wore makeup and cute clothes and talked about boys. I was pretty sure the boys were talking about them too. Especially Kim—the girl with long blond hair, thick eyelashes, and the cutest dimples when she smiled.

As we unpacked, Kim told her friends that she preferred showering at night, and they all agreed. Apparently, it was far better to shower at night. But I hadn't planned to shower at all. This was *camp*! Since I hadn't packed a towel or shampoo, I began silently fretting about what Kim and her friends would think by day three about the girl who didn't shower morning *or* evening.

When the girls came back from the showers, I watched with interest as Kim rolled her damp hair into pink sponge rollers. Then in the morning I almost gasped. Kim's long blond hair had been transformed into big, beautiful curls that now bounced along on her shoulders as she moved. I was intrigued, to say the least. I was also filled with hopeful glee, for though it was glaringly obvious that I did not measure up to Kim and her friends, she had just disclosed her secret to enviable beauty. *Sponge rollers!*

I endured three showerless, out-of-place days at camp, wishing I could just find Kath and go back to passing notes and giggling in sleeping bags. Yet somehow, I knew those days were over. I returned home with a new determination to grow up and reinvent myself. First order of business? Sponge rollers.

My mom was kind enough to get me some, and that night I showered and rolled up my damp, shortish brown hair in the pink rollers—just as Kim had done. The next morning I pulled the rollers out and ran to the mirror. This time I *did* gasp—but not because my reflection revealed anything enviable or beautiful. I looked as if I had been electrocuted!

Sixth grade camp was a turning point. My life went from light-hearted to awkward. From carefree to insecure. From happy-go-lucky to sick-to-your-stomach inadequate. Literally overnight, my eyes fluttered open. I saw something which had been previously hidden. A dimension I had been oblivious to. A whole new world was opening up. The world of comparison.

COMPARISON LINES

Go back in time and take a mental snapshot of yourself in middle school. In your hand is a glass measuring cup filled with your gifts, aptitudes, and talents. Your personality is mixed in, along with your family background and experiences. Your cup is overflowing with potential . . . and that potential is exactly what Satan wants to steal, kill, and destroy. He wants to steal your very life from you.

Satan does not fight fair. He doesn't wait until a girl is old enough to process her experiences objectively. Before she even has a chance to figure out who she is, he entices her to measure what's in her cup against somebody else's. In fact, I think Satan organizes his armies to attack just as a girl—blinking in bewilderment—first notices that there even *are* lines on the side of her measuring cup.

I don't have proof of this, of course. But when I watch an eleven- or twelve-year-old girl go from passing silly notes, hugging her friends, and including everyone in her games to suddenly becoming ensnared in sexting, cutting, and mean-girl tactics, I can almost see the demons prowling. And how do they attack her? What is their tactic? They point to the lines on her measuring cup and entice her to compare.

Think back to your middle school self. Were there times you didn't feel you measured up? Maybe your volleyball serve was weak or your clothes weren't stylish. Maybe a boy broke up with you and bragged about it. As you measured and found yourself lacking, what happened?

Did you develop new insecurities or self-consciousness? Did you become more me-focused? Think also of the times you compared and came out on top. Maybe your grades were higher or your legs were thinner. Maybe the boys paid more attention to you. As you measured yourself against others and found yourself to be "better than," what happened? Did you gain a sense of self-importance or arrogance? Did you become more me-focused?

Satan didn't care whether you were the girl comparing up or comparing down. Both inferiority and superiority lead to me-focused bondage which can last decades. All Satan has to do is keep wickedly pointing to the lines and tempting us all to compare.

PAUL'S PERSPECTIVE

Do you doubt that Satan has anything to do with your comparison struggles? Paul didn't. In 2 Corinthians 10–11, when Paul was responding to some critics in the church who were picking him apart and trying to make him feel inferior, he began his response by talking about spiritual warfare (2 Cor. 10:4). So Paul discerns what is behind these comparison attacks. He looks beyond these opponents who are holding their measuring cups next to his and pointing at the lines, and he recognizes the work of the enemy. "When they measure themselves by one another and compare themselves with one another, they are without understanding," Paul said (2 Cor. 10:12). Paul's opponents didn't get that there was a spiritual war and they were part of it, but Paul did, and he was ready to respond accordingly.

I have to be honest. I love this truth that flows from Paul's pen, but he was a grown man trained in theology and logic. What about a middle schooler? I hope it makes you angry to think of Satan lobbing comparison attacks at your naïve, middle school self. But I hope it makes you even *more* angry to think of him keeping you in bondage decades later, using the same tired strategy.

It's time to follow Paul's lead and acknowledge that measure-up comparison is not a game; it's a strategy of war used by Satan, who has been our adversary since childhood.

WHAT SATAN WANTS

The Bible doesn't give much backstory for Satan and his demons. In the same way that I tell my kids detailed stories about their dad and not old boyfriends, the Bible tells the story of Jesus and his church, not the petty rival who keeps trying to steal the bride.

The bits we do have of Satan's story are blurred into poems and prophesies, but here's what we can gather. Satan once had rank and position in heaven, but in his discontent he wanted his throne lifted higher. He loathed being less than God, so he set out to lift himself up, saying, "I will be like the Most High."[2] See that comparison word, "like"?

Satan's undoing began with comparison. He measured himself against God, which, for a created being, was audacious. Satan's pride wasn't tolerated by God, and he fell from heaven like a streak of lightning (Luke 10:18). When he landed on earth, it was not with new meekness. Satan is a liar and the truth has no place in him, so he lives out the delusion that he is somehow God's rival. Still today, he roams the earth with dogged resolve to challenge God's preeminence. And how does Satan attack God? By hurting and destroying us. He sees us as pawns to prove his blasphemous point.

Many times, we're foolishly oblivious to this cosmic battle playing out in the heavenly realms. We stumble into comparison, thinking only of our own selfish agendas, and Satan is fine with that. From day one with Eve, Satan has been suggesting that we cut God out of the story and slide up onto the throne of our lives without him (Gen. 3:5). Our enemy is content to stay out of sight, whispering his measure-up messages, then grinning wickedly as we begin to march around like mini imperialists, wanting to be more and have more. Our house is not big enough. Our waist is not small enough. Our promotion is not high enough. Satan also enjoys it when we pout and cower like *affronted* mini imperialists until no house is big enough. No waist size is small enough. No promotion is high enough. Little by little, we start to resemble Satan, back when he was insisting on a higher throne—and Satan counts this as a win. He wants us to ignore God and fold into ourselves, since this causes our destruction. But Jesus came to show us another way.

An Upside-Down Cup

If Jesus had a measuring cup, it would be full to the brim and overflowing. In fact, it would be impossible to find a cup that could contain all his worth and still fit inside the universe. In heaven, with unveiled glory, the supreme value of God's Son is uncontested. His worth is simply beyond compare. But on earth, Jesus didn't concern himself with proving this.

Jesus's arrival was not punctuated with royal fanfare. The night he was born, his mother laid him in a manger because there was no room for them in the inn (Luke 2:7). His dad was a simple carpenter with no wealth or status. Even Jesus's physical body was average and unimpressive. Isaiah 53:2 says, "There was nothing beautiful or majestic about his appearance, nothing to attract us to him" (NLT).

Jesus spent plenty of time among "the least of these," healing their sickness and disease. And he invested in those who had wealth and power too. Jesus shared meals and conversations with people who were deeply sinful and devoutly religious. He shared his life with twelve ordinary disciples, demonstrating foot-washing humility. Jesus modeled his upside-down kingdom by lowering himself, not exalting himself. Jesus came, "not to be served but to serve, and to give his life as a ransom for many" (Matt. 20:28).

Only a human being could give his life to atone fully for the sins of humanity. That's the whole reason Jesus became a man. And only a completely righteous substitute could be pierced for *our* transgressions and crushed for *our* iniquities and thereby cancel the record of our sin (Isa. 53:5; Col. 2:14). Only God's Son had the power to rise from the dead in triumph over Satan and his armies, putting them to "open shame" (Col. 2:15). Only Jesus could serve us in this way, and that's exactly what he did.

Jesus took his measuring cup and unequivocally focused on the spout. Philippians 2:7 says Jesus "emptied himself, by taking the form of a servant, being born in the likeness of men." Isaiah 53:12 says that Jesus "poured out his soul to death." From his moment of birth until his moment of death, Jesus had complete disregard for the lines on his measuring cup. He turned his measuring cup upside down.

TIPPING MY CUP

When Jesus invites us to follow him and live under his rule, it's not with promises that he will finally fulfill our measure-up dreams. Jesus wants us to be great—but according to *his* kingdom's value system, not the world's. **Satan points to the lines; King Jesus points to the spout.** Satan's rule has a definite expiration date, but Jesus's rule will be eternal. We have to decide which ruler we will emulate: The evil one who is still trying to lift his throne higher and will one day be thrown to "the bottomless pit" (Rev. 9:1)? Or the righteous one who, in the most extravagant display of humility the world has ever known, went willingly to the cross and has been highly exalted and given "the name that is above every name" (Phil. 2:9)?

In Jesus's kingdom, the great ones are those who serve. Whoever humbles herself will be exalted, and whoever exalts herself will be humbled (Matt. 23:12). We're invited today to live the way we'll wish we had when the upside-down kingdom is fully instated—to bring glory to God and serve others like Jesus did, to focus on the spout. But "someday greatness" isn't our only reward. There's another, more immediate benefit. If we want to shut down comparison's lies and live-by-the-lines temptation, all we have to do is turn our attention to the spout.

When I tip my measuring cup, the lines become beautifully irrelevant. When I walk into a room asking, "Who can I serve here? What needs can I meet? What do I have to offer? Where can I pour myself out?" I have a completely different outlook than when I measure myself against everyone I see. Instead of being preoccupied with what I look like, how I just sounded, or what everyone is thinking, by pouring myself out I *free* myself from measure-up comparison. I am more confident, less self-conscious. I'm more joyful, less troubled. I'm more content, less driven by perfectionism. Living by the spout is the way to be "me-free"!

THE LINES OR THE SPOUT?

Take inventory of your life and the way you relate to others. Are you more focused on the lines or the spout? Put an X by each characteristic that describes you:

Living by the Me-Focused Lines
___ I am privately jealous of others' successes.

___ I am frustrated and sometimes humiliated by my own personal limitations or mistakes.

___ I have excessive ambition to prove myself or get ahead.

___ I'm a perfectionist at work, with fitness, in parenting, etc.

___ I'm often disgusted with others who aren't living as I think they should.

___ I feel worthless because I don't measure up.

___ I am self-conscious and obsess over what others think.

___ I tally up my accomplishments and readily display them on social media.

___ I isolate myself and pull away because I'm insecure or intimidated.

___ It's hard for me to be authentic and vulnerable, so I lack true community.

Living by the Others-Focused Spout
___ I stay quiet about my successes and am careful to be approachable.

___ I don't worry much about the approval or disapproval of others.

___ I am comfortable with my limits and just do what I can.

___ I use my gifts and strengths to lift other people up.

___ I am happy to serve humbly behind the scenes or in front—whatever is most helpful.

___ I don't seek recognition; those who serve alongside me know this.

___ I have a teachable spirit when differences arise.

___ I am careful to put the interests of others ahead of my own.

___ I enjoy unity and harmony in relationships.

___ I experience community with a diverse group of people.

Do you, like I do, find far more descriptions of yourself on that first list—and less on the second—than you'd like? If so, could it be that we've been deceived? Friend, let's leave behind this dark measure-up world. Let's escape to the kingdom where people live humbly by the spout, not the lines. Let's follow our Jesus and be finally free.

≈ Which "Living by the Lines" characteristics are most convicting or troubling to you? Make a list of what has been stolen, killed, or destroyed in your life as you've measured yourself against others.

≈ In your Bible (or using printed verses), read Isaiah's prophecy of the coming Christ in Isaiah 53 and, with a downward arrow (↓), mark all the ways that Jesus ultimately emptied or humbled himself. Write a prayer, using some of your favorite phrases from Isaiah 53, thanking Jesus for pouring himself out with such beautiful humility.

≈ Read Philippians 2:3–11 and list the ways Jesus emptied himself and became a servant. Write down one way God is asking you to "empty" yourself. How might this free you from superior or inferior comparison?

For Meditation: Mark 10:45

The Son of Man came not to be served but to serve, and
to give his life as a ransom for many.

When I tip my measuring cup and pour myself out to others, the lines become irrelevant. *Lord, help me to find freedom from comparison by humbling myself as you did.*

Lesson 2: Green-Eyed Wisdom
Read James 3:13–4:10 and 1 Kings 3

"WELL, GOODIE FOR you," I said with a sneer at my phone. I had just read a friend's post about how kind and generous her daughter had been to her siblings. On some other day her photo and caption wouldn't have annoyed me. But on *this* day, after breaking up several sibling fights over who took whose jacket or phone or turn, I found my friend's celebration of her daughter's virtue rather annoying.

Jealousy, selfish ambition, and rivalry are the natural results of comparison. That's obvious, right? You can't become jealous or selfishly ambitious without first focusing on your measuring cup lines. But here's the part that might not be obvious. You have an enemy who *wants* you to become bitterly jealous and who *plots* to lure you into selfish ambition. The scheming forces of evil want to entice you to compare.

Please don't take my word for it. I'd like you to make the connection yourself between jealousy (the resentment when you don't measure up) or selfish ambition (the aspiration to get ahead) with Satan's agenda in the world. In the verses printed below:

- Circle any Comparison Girl tendencies or temptations.
- Underline references to Satan, his regime, or his rule.

If your heart is one that bleeds dark streams of jeal-

ousy and selfishness, do not be so proud that you

ignore your depraved state. The wisdom of this world

should never be mistaken for heavenly wisdom; it orig-

inates below in the earthly realms, with the demons.

Any place where you find jealousy and selfish ambi-

tion, you will discover chaos and evil thriving under its

rule. (James 3:14–16 VOICE[3])

Do you see the ties? **Our jealousy and selfish ambition serve as "Satan was here" graffiti on the walls of our lives.** When I pout sullenly because someone else has more in her measuring cup, saying, "Why her, not me?" or when I drive myself to outdo others, saying, "I must prove that I have more than she does!" then I'm living evidence that evil is still thriving.

BITTER JEALOUSY

If you had told me that I could become bitter and jealous of my friend Melissa, I would have fiercely denied it. I love Melissa dearly—especially because of the way she helped me through a painful disappointment several years back. I had worked for nine months pouring my heart into writing my first book, and then two weeks before the manuscript was due, the book got canceled. It wasn't personal, I was told. Big Publications was dissolving the department that had produced the Amazing[4] line of Bible studies that my book was to be part of. But still, for me it was disheartening.

Melissa took long walks with me in the weeks to follow, praying over me and giving me encouragement and support. She was incredibly kind and generous during this time. Then a few months later Melissa called with some news. Big Publications wanted to publish her next book, yet she was hesitant because of me. "Shannon, if you want me to turn it down, I will," she said. I was amazed at my friend's willingness to lay down a dream if it might hurt me. What sweet humility! Her kindness and concern made it easy for me to give my wholehearted blessing. "Of *course* you should take this opportunity!" I said.

Then several days after Melissa's phone call, I received two emails.

The first one informed me that my book had been rejected by another publisher, which brought a wave of disappointment and made the second email harder. Melissa was announcing to friends that she had just signed a contract with Big Publications. This didn't surprise me, of course, but one detail did. I hadn't realized that Melissa's book was slotted to be part of the Amazing line—which apparently wasn't being dissolved as I had thought.

My friend had been so selfless and kind, yet my enemy still used this little detail like a powerful undertow, pulling me into the bitter waters of comparison. *Why did the Amazing line have room for Melissa's book but not mine? Why was she being accepted when I was rejected? Why did God want her book published and not mine?* I stared at my computer screen, gulping jealousy, hot tears ready to spill.

Then came a message, clear and strong. *You should pull back from Melissa. Just delete the email and withdraw. It hurts too much.*

It was the voice of the enemy using jealousy in an attempt to destroy my relationship with Melissa.

WISDOM FROM BELOW

Satan loves it when God's people become sudden enemies with each other. He loves to create division, strife, mistrust, and disharmony between a Comparison Girl and her close friend. He tells her that outrage is normal. Protecting herself is necessary. Of *course* she has to pull away from this person she's suddenly jealous of. What other choice does she have?

But jealousy is always fed by the wisdom from below. James 3:14–15 says, "If you have bitter jealousy and selfish ambition in your hearts . . . this is not the wisdom that comes down from above, but is earthly, unspiritual, demonic."

Wisdom—whether from above or below—is always saying, "You should do *this*." It wants to take your hand and lead you in a direction. So how can you tell these two wisdoms apart? Here's a clear distinction. Wisdom from below says, "You should do what's good for *you*." It leads you down the path of self-focus, self-protection, and self-promotion. But wisdom from above says, "You should do not only what's good for you but also what's good for others."[5] Do you hear the hints of this me-free mindset in the way James describes heaven's wisdom? He says, "The wisdom from above is first pure, then peaceable, gentle, open to reason, full of mercy and good fruits, impartial and sincere" (James 3:17). When you're led by the wisdom from above, you find a way to be at peace with other people. You're reasonable. You show mercy. You're generous. But when jealousy is tugging at your wrist, it often leads you down a path of isolation—away from the very people who might have offered you the most support. Ironically, the wisdom from below, which is markedly me-focused, is designed to destroy you. And one way it does so is by creating division and pulling you away from friends.

Consider how jealousy divided the two women in the following Bible story.

SOLOMON'S SWORD

Solomon had just taken the throne when two women came to him with their conflict. They were housemates, each with a newborn baby, and one mother had tragically rolled over on her son and suffocated him in the night. When she awoke and realized the tragedy, she snuck to her roommate's bedside and swapped her deceased baby for the live one. When the second mother awoke, she was horrified to find the lifeless child at her side. Then she was equally horrified to realize this baby wasn't hers.

With no witnesses, the two mothers brought their dispute to King Solomon, who had just been given the epic opportunity of asking God for one gift. What had he asked for? Wisdom (1 Kings 3:7, 9). So, newly endowed with wisdom from above, Solomon presented the mothers with a "solution" that brilliantly drew out both the extreme selfishness and extreme selflessness of the two mothers. He called for the baby to be sliced in half.

Immediately, the true mother said, "Oh my lord, give her the living child, and by no means put him to death" (1 Kings 3:26). See her selflessness? She would rather give her son away than see him die, and by this, Solomon knew she was innocent. But look also at the extreme me-focus of the guilty mother.

No doubt she was horrified to find her lifeless baby in the night. What a sorrow to bear! But to watch the other mother have the joy when her own joy had been snatched away was equally unbearable. She decided that kidnapping the other baby—or even watching him die—was more favorable than enduring the bitter stabs of jealousy. The guilty mother offers a chilling display of listening to the wisdom that says, "You should do what's good for *you*."

This green-eyed wisdom from below takes our hand and leads us to make war on anyone enjoying a newborn delight. "You shouldn't be the one enduring the still coldness of sorrow," it hisses. "She should!" These demonic messages of extreme self-focus whispered into our Comparison Girl ears lead to vicious rivalries, coveting, hatred, and relational war (see James 4:1–3). And when the dust settles, there's a chasm between those of us who should have been close friends.

RESISTING MY ENEMY, NOT MY FRIEND

My friend Melissa and I have something in common with these two women. We share the same enemy who snarls at our friendship and leaps at the opportunity to divide us with his dark wisdom.

The day I opened Melissa's email, the temptation to be jealous and withdraw in self-protectiveness was strong, but God inside me was stronger. Melissa had been a true, selfless friend to me. She had even offered to forgo her own blessing out of humble deference to me. I would be crazy to push away a friend like her!

I've learned that it's urgent to settle matters like this right away, so in quick desperation I cried, "Lord, help me resist the temptation to selfishly withdraw from our friendship. Help me to rejoice with Melissa instead and celebrate all the ways you're using her!" Right then and there, I clicked "reply" and typed a heartfelt note to Melissa, promising to cheer her on every step of the way with her new book project and support her in any way I could.

Do you know what happened next? As that email left my screen, so did every trace of jealousy. I had resisted the enemy, and he had fled (James 4:7). The wisdom from above had set me free.

Oh, dear friend, I want you to have this freedom. How will you refuse to operate out of jealousy, me-focus, and self-defense today? Who will you selflessly cheer on and celebrate? How will you resist the devil and live me-*free*?

≈ In your journal, describe any interpersonal conflicts or strained relationships that have been negatively impacted by jealousy or selfish ambition. Then read James 4:1–10 one time for each situation. Write down any of the phrases God uses to convict or comfort you. How is God asking you to respond?

≈ Read James 3:17–18 and list the characteristics of wisdom from above. Now choose one difficult situation or relationship that most tempts you to vehemently protect yourself. Write out the wisdom from above that most applies to your situation, beginning each statement with "I should . . ." Which piece of advice from God will you put into practice today?

≈ In 1 Kings 3:16–27, how did Solomon's wisdom help identify guilt? Allow this wisdom to reveal your own heart regarding the conflicts you've already listed. How would you respond if one of these people died or was hurt? Repent of any extreme selfishness or jealousy that God reveals in your heart.

For Meditation: James 3:14–15

But if you have bitter jealousy and selfish ambition in your hearts . . . this is not the wisdom that comes down from above.

Wisdom from below says, "You should do what's good for *you*." Wisdom from above says, "You should do what is good for others." *God, help me to resist the devil by refusing to operate out of jealousy, me-focus, or self-defense.*

Lesson 3: Pride-Thickened Comparison Walls
Read 1 Peter 5:6–11

I HEARD ABOUT a woman named Penny who decided to self-publish a book on how to make a million dollars. In reality, however, Penny doesn't have a million dollars; she doesn't even have enough to make ends meet. So now she's created a problem for herself since it might raise suspicion about her credibility if "millionaire" Penny took a job as a waitress or opened a daycare. So Penny's only way to make money is by selling a book that says she doesn't *need* to make money.

What would drive someone to fabricate a story like this and put herself in such a Comparison Girl conundrum? Lots of reasons, maybe, but I'm guessing the most basic one is pride. Not a healthy pride—like when you take pride in your work or an accomplishment. I'm guessing it's the unhealthy kind of pride that wants to show the world you have more in your measuring cup than somebody else does.

WHY COMPARISON FEEDS PRIDE

As Comparison Girls, our pride takes many forms. For instance:

- Envious pride says, "I wish I was great like her."
- Jealous pride says, "I'm angry because she is great."
- Haughty pride says, "I'm so happy that I'm great."
- Insecure pride says, "I'm ashamed because I'm not great."

And in each instance, our pride is fed by comparing ourselves with others. C. S. Lewis writes:

> We say that people are proud of being rich, or clever, or good-looking, but they are not. They are proud of being richer, or cleverer, or better-looking than others.

If everyone else became equally rich, or clever, or good-
looking there would be nothing to be proud about. It
is the comparison that makes you proud: The pleasure
of being above the rest.[6]

It is also comparison that creates *wounded* pride—or the displeasure
of being below the rest. Pride is always asking, *How do I measure up?* Pride
might be glancing around the room, but its preoccupation is with self.
It loathes being exposed as "less than" or "beneath" other people.

We see comparison-driven pride in Satan's story. Remember that it
was Satan's disdain for being beneath God which caused him to be cast
from heaven. "It was through pride that the devil became the devil," says
Lewis.[7] So as we choose to follow King Jesus and reject our Comparison
Girl ways, we've got to think carefully about our pride.

THE DANGER OF COMPARISON WALLS

After publishing her millionaire story, Penny moved far away and
put lots of relational distance between herself and those who knew her.
The distance was essential for maintaining her facade—especially since
Penny doesn't really own the sprawling mansion or the Ferrari in her
Instagram photos. In order to stand beside them in her photos, she has
to stand far away from the people who know better.

Consider what Penny's choices have cost her—especially relation-
ally. She has chosen such an isolated life. But then, I have to consider
the cost of my own comparison-fed pride. In real life or online, when I
edit out the uncomplimentary and present you with a full-measuring-
cup version of my life (helped by good lighting and great angles), I only
thicken the invisible comparison walls that divide us. Walls like these
might make me feel safe, but they're actually dangerous. They put me
at greater risk.

First Peter 5:8 says, "Be sober-minded; be watchful. Your adversary
the devil prowls around like a roaring lion, seeking someone to devour."
Peter, the disciple of Jesus who wrote this, knew something about Satan's
attacks. As Peter penned these words about standing firm against the

enemy, I wonder if he was picturing his own trembling heart, being sifted by the devil, that night he warmed himself by the fire during Jesus's arrest.

Peter's comparison-fed pride surfaced repeatedly, but one of the most blatant occasions was when Peter told Jesus that the others might fall away but he never would (Mark 14:29). Peter was always trying to differentiate himself from the other disciples. He wanted to be known as the strong one. The devoted one. The superior one. But as you know, lions target the isolated individual, not those packed tightly into a group.

Just hours after Peter told Jesus he would never fall away, he stood alone beside that fire and denied even knowing Jesus (Luke 22:31–34, 55–57)—which makes me wonder. What would have happened if Peter had linked arms with the other disciples in solidarity that night? Perhaps we'd have a story of eleven disciples "standing firm in one spirit, with one mind striving side by side for the faith of the gospel, and not frightened in anything by [their] opponents" (Phil. 1:27–28).

The only way we can stand firm is side by side, as a flock—not in isolation behind our comparison walls. **Humility, which cultivates community, protects us against Satan's attacks.** With your Bible open to 1 Peter 5:1–11, look with me at the words of Peter as he cares for the flock of Jesus (John 21:17) by warning against comparison-fed pride.

Humility Is My Safe Place

As one of Jesus's sheep, I'm most safe when I humble myself—crouched low and tucked small under God's mighty hand (1 Peter 5:6). In that safe place among the rest of the flock, I don't have to worry about whether I seem small, inferior, or flawed in the eyes of others. Humility allows me to cast my measure-up anxieties on God (v. 7), knowing that I am not abandoned; I am cared for.

The Devil Wants to Get Fed

Satan's roar in my ear often sounds like, "What will people think? Don't let them know that your measuring cup isn't full!" With my ears still ringing, I do things like dropping humble brags into conversations or inflating the truth. As I steal out from my safe place under God's hand to take matters into my own, Satan smells my pride and licks his lips (v. 8). His ego gets fed every time I step out to defend, protect, or lift myself up—since I'm obviously saying God can't be trusted.

On the other hand, when I plug my ears to Satan's roars by trusting God's promises to one day restore, confirm, strengthen, and establish me (vv. 9–10), I'm able to turn my focus from the lines to the spout. And that's when my enemy goes hungry.

I'm Not Being Singled Out

Resisting the enemy involves refuting the idea that I'm the only one facing opposition (v. 9). When I think I'm the only one (another form of pride), I'm tempted to either be ashamed (because obviously no one else is as weak or pathetic as I am) or I'm tempted to pity myself (because obviously God spared everyone this grief except me). Notice these comparison-generated lies?

Here's what's true. I'm part of a family of suffering people. All of us struggle. All of us need each other. It's my me-focused pride that asks, "What will the others think?" and causes me to shrink back in isolation, making myself more vulnerable to Satan's attacks. Me-free humility, on the other hand, cultivates family community. I'm far stronger when I face the enemy's attacks in solidarity rather than alone.

I Need to Wear Humility Like Clothes

All of us need to clothe ourselves with humility (v. 5). All means all. One person's pride puts everyone's humility at risk. I need to get dressed in humility the same way I get dressed to meet a friend for lunch—to purposefully put humility on. Of course, Satan suggests other wardrobe options. He generously hands out cloaks and wraps, woven with stiff threads of pride.

Pride clothes are impressive from a distance, but when I wear them, I feel prickly, which tends to make me keep my distance and constantly check the mirror. And I tempt my friends to do the same—which puts all of us in danger out there alone. There's an enemy prowling around and roaring in our ears, and we are safest *together*. So I need to strip myself of pride and get dressed in the warm, soft, beautiful layers of humility, which is the perfect attire for cozy fellowship.

THE PROTECTION OF HUMILITY

In his book *The Freedom of Self-Forgetfulness*, Tim Keller says, "The essence of gospel-humility is not thinking more of myself or thinking less of myself, it is thinking of myself less."[8] Humility frees us to stop thinking about the lines. It allows us to truly see other people, rather than being wrapped up in how they see us. In humility, we tip our measuring cups to serve other people, rather than holding up our cups in the best light to prove that we have more. **Pride thickens our comparison walls, but humility collapses them.**

I got to experience this phenomenon recently when I was out to lunch with a group of friends. We were sharing updates, and when it was my turn, I could have cropped out the ugly and shared the beautiful, but instead I told my friends what had really been going on in my heart that week.

Several days prior, someone I greatly admire had posted a negative review of something I'd written, which validated all my fears. *Nobody else gets critiques like this. Should I just quit? Is everyone wishing I would?* For days, I had struggled through the fog of shame and self-doubt. But I shared with my friends that as I sought the Lord, he had showed me something new: My perfectionism was drenched with pride.

Why did this review matter so much? Why was I under the impression that the whole world was staring at it? My wounded spirit was evidence that my eyes were too fixated on *me*. I needed the humility to accept that I was just learning, like everybody else, and get back to the work of growing and improving.

After sharing about my less-than-five-star review with my friends, they offered encouragement, perspective, and support. But there was another benefit coming as well.

COLLAPSING WALLS

After lunch, as my friend Julie and I walked out together, she thanked me for being vulnerable. She shared that as the others had been giving updates around the table, feelings of inferiority had begun rising inside her. *These women are having such amazing opportunities*, she thought. *Why haven't doors like these opened for me yet?* But when I shared about my measure-up struggle, Julie felt less alone—which was the purpose of our lunch date in the first place.

The next day, I got a call from Julie. She had just received a scathing email from her brother, who was outraged because of how Julie had framed her life story in a recent article. He called her a self-victimizing, sanctimonious liar, which was both devastating and unfair. Julie had shared a painful memory from her past to encourage hurting people,[9] but now she was the one being hurt.

I said, "Julie, this attack from your brother is also an attack from your enemy, and you need to *resist*! You were not driven to vindicate yourself or play the victim in this article. You were driven to serve other people. *That's* the truth." Satan was roaring in my friend's ear, and I was reminding her to stay in her safe place, under the mighty hand of God.

DEFENDING OURSELVES AS A COMMUNITY

Researcher Brené Brown says that vulnerability is the birthplace of connection.[10] When we talk about our fears, struggles, pain, and difficulties rather than trying to hide from each other in self-protectiveness, our comparison walls crumble. When someone is vulnerable and authentic, the group leans in. Empathy, compassion, partnership, and authenticity are invited to the table.

Now, I'm not talking about a self-focused pity party. Nor am I suggesting we one-up each other with failure stories so we can all feel better about ourselves. Humility doesn't manifest itself in either of those ways. It says, "I'm not going to showboat my successes or hide my weaknesses. I'm just offering you the real me because I'm interested in knowing the real you." True humility finds the courage to be vulnerable—which is how community is built. And it is in humility-clad community that we defend ourselves against enemy attack.

Look in with me on that restaurant gathering with my friends. Can you almost picture the enemy there, circling our table with his mouth watering? What if we had all worn our pride garments, with puffed chests and look-at-me agendas? What if we had put up comparison walls and Julie had left the table feeling even more alone? She was about to face an attack, and isolation was the last thing she needed.

As we interact with others, there's often far more at stake than we realize. No wonder Peter told us to be sober-minded and watchful, and ward off the pride that isolates and divides. Find someone to turn to and say, "Let's not live behind walls. Let's be vulnerable, honest, humility-clad people who welcome each other to the circle." For the circle is where we defend ourselves against attack.

≈ Which relationships in your life have become distant or strained because of comparison? How has this made you more vulnerable to Satan's lies? Write down one way you will courageously choose humble vulnerability and invite connection.

≈ Which of the truths from 1 Peter 5:5–11 is God challenging you with? How will you respond?

≈ Read Philippians 1:15–18. What signs do you see that the enemy is attacking Paul? How is Paul an example of the instructions in 1 Peter 5:6–7?

≈ Choose one phrase from Philippians 1:27–30 that inspires you to defend yourself with Christian community.

For Meditation: Philippians 1:27

Standing firm in one spirit, with one mind striving side by side for the faith of the gospel.

Comparison-fed pride keeps us from connecting, but in humility-clad community we defend ourselves against enemy attack. *Lord, give me courage to be vulnerable enough to connect with those who will take their stand with me against the enemy.*

Lesson 4: A Rival Named Jesus
Read Luke 3:1–17 and John 3:22–36

ONE SUMMER AS a college-aged camp counselor, I was thumbing through the stack of photos that had just been processed (this was before digital photos) and held one up to show several staff members beside me. "Isn't this a great picture of Uncle Carl and me?" I said.

"It's good of *you*, but it's horrible of Carl," one of the guys responded. Instantly embarrassed, I turned back and realized I hadn't even taken a good look at Uncle Carl—the older gentleman who helped with camp maintenance. Obviously, I had seen him in the photo, but my eyes had rested on *me*. As I lifted the photo up to show others, I had wanted them to see *me*. I was stuck in selfie mode before there even was such a thing.

Decades later—now that "selfie" is an actual word—I hate to admit that I'm often still stuck in selfie mode. I swipe through group shots and landscape shots, expanding each one but hardly even seeing the beautiful people or scenery around me. My eyes scan the photo looking for one criterion: Is this photo flattering of me? If not, the delete icon is very handy.

Me-focus like this might be commonplace in our measure-up world, but it's unbecoming in the kingdom of heaven. And **it's particularly unbecoming when we overfocus on ourselves and forget to notice Jesus.**

JOHN'S DISREGARD FOR THE LINES

In the chapters ahead, we'll see Jesus respond to lots of people who are stuck in selfie mode. We'll meet rich people, religious people, sinful people, and disciples who are comparing and measuring themselves against each other—all oblivious to the fact that they're interacting with the King of Kings and Lord of Lords (Rev. 19:16). But Jesus encountered one guy who stood apart from the rest. In fact, Jesus said that among those born to women, there was none greater than this man (Luke 7:28)—which is quite a comparison statement coming from Jesus.

Who was this man and what made him great? He was John the Baptist, and his beautiful humility and deference to Jesus are what inoculated him from measure-up comparison. John didn't naturally measure up by the world's standards. He wore weird camel-hair clothes and ate locusts. But then overnight, John became a wilderness wonder, with people making the trek out to hear him preach: "Repent, for the kingdom of heaven is at hand" (Matt. 3:2). Amazingly, the people responded to John's message and one by one dipped into the waters of repentance, then came up with fresh commitment to turn from their sin. Revival was breaking out, and many were suggesting that John might be the Christ (Luke 3:15).

Many would've become swept up in such instant popularity, but not John. He was quick to set the record straight. No, he wasn't the Christ; he was just the one preparing the way *for* the Christ. In comparison, John didn't even feel worthy to bend down and untie Jesus's sandal (John 1:20, 27)—which is saying something when you consider how Middle Easterners (then and now) consider shoes to be dreadfully unclean.[11]

John saw an expansive distance between his own status and that of Jesus. His aim from the beginning was not to turn people toward himself but to direct them straight to Christ. Then one day, this happened— literally. John recognized Jesus for who he was and announced, "Behold, the Lamb of God, who takes away the sin of the world!" (John 1:29). And just like that, people began turning to Jesus. John 1:35–37 reads:

> John was standing with two of his disciples, and he looked at Jesus as he walked by and said, "Behold the Lamb of God!" The two disciples heard him say this, and they followed Jesus.

Did you catch that? John's two disciples abruptly turned to become Jesus's two disciples. And they weren't the only ones. After identifying Jesus as the Christ, John's crowds immediately thinned. His popularity cooled. His numbers began to drop in direct correlation with Jesus's rise.

Back away and think of this scene from Satan's perspective. People are repenting, revival is breaking out, and Jesus has just arrived to save sinners and bring them into his kingdom. Satan is vehemently opposed to all of the above, but how can he unravel it? Ahh . . . there it is. John's notoriety has just been eclipsed by Jesus's, which creates a situation ripe for comparison. And that's when Satan readies himself to pounce.

We can't be definitive about Satan's involvement, but this next part of the story has "Satan was here" graffiti all over it.

He Must Increase

Just as people are turning to Jesus, a Jewish leader[12] showed up to heckle John's disciples about purification laws. For a while now, the religious leaders had been watching John carefully—threatened by the way people were flocking to him as if *he* was greater than *they* were. Perhaps this religious heckler came to challenge John's baptisms and prove that the sacrifice system at the temple is sufficient; we aren't told. But then as the heckler is brought to John, he shifts gears.

Pointing across the river at the line forming near Jesus's baptismal spot, the heckler says, "Look, [Jesus] is baptizing, and all are going to him" (John 3:26).

That they were. The people who had yesterday been flocking to John were now flocking to Jesus. In a moment, John's measuring cup—filled with popularity and status—was emptied. And there was the heckler, pointing to the lines.

Remember that Satan's mission, at that moment, is to kill Jesus, and he's already recruiting the accomplices we'd least expect—the religious leaders. This heckler (who is part of that group) has been influenced by the wisdom from below, and he's come to infect John with the same measure-up jealousy and selfish promotion, but John refuses to fall like the next domino.

In response, John did not hang his head in shame. He did not sulk. He did not territorially stamp his foot. Instead, John looked across the river at the people turning to Jesus and said, "He must increase, but I must decrease" (John 3:30). And in so doing, he displayed the upside-down greatness of heaven.

COMPETING WITH JESUS

Do you want Jesus to increase? Do you want people to see and turn to him? Do you want his kingdom to expand? I'm guessing you'd probably be willing to join me in saying, "He must increase!" But what about the next part? Are you willing to "decrease" for Jesus's sake?

As Comparison Girls, we don't often think of ourselves as "competing" with Jesus. We think of our "rivals" as the ones who might get the promotion, get the solo, get the guy, and so on. Yet here's what we must recognize. Whenever our "look at me" craving is stronger than our "look at Jesus" craving, when *we* want to be lifted up more than we want Jesus to be, when we want others to admire us more than we want them to admire our Lord, that is when we have made Jesus our rival. Even if we simply ignore Jesus, saying, "I must increase!" it is clear that we are being influenced by the subtle voice of our enemy, who works tirelessly to infect us with his own jealousy, pride, and selfish ambition.

There is coming a day, the Bible tells us, when a man indwelled with Satan (the Antichrist) will exalt himself to such extravagant heights that he will slide into God's seat in the temple and proclaim himself to *be* God (2 Thess. 2:4). This audacious self-exaltation is what got Satan kicked out of heaven in the first place, and it's what will finalize his demise. "And then [Satan] will be revealed, whom the Lord Jesus will kill with the breath of his mouth and bring to nothing by the appearance of his coming" (v. 8). Did you catch that? Jesus will show up and breathe on the guy, and this Satan-indwelled man will be annihilated! Who do you think will be exalted *then*?

Friends, our Jesus will not tolerate rivalry. He will not share his glory. He welcomes us into his kingdom as our King, or not at all. Jesus knows that we only flourish when we bow to his kingship—not when we march around like mini imperialists, expanding our own little crumbling empires.

And how does the upside-down kingdom expand? When individuals humble themselves as John did, exalting Jesus and saying, "He must increase and I must decrease."

OFF TO THE SIDE

John offered an interesting word picture in response to that pointing heckler. He compared himself to a groomsman and Jesus to a groom. All along John has been saying he isn't the Christ; he's only the one who comes before the Christ—the way a groomsman comes down the aisle before the groom. Wouldn't it be ludicrous, John said, for him to feel threatened because the bride is turning her attention to the groom? As the people turn to Jesus's voice, it's like seeing a bride turn to hear her groom pledge his love. Who would begrudge *that*? So John doesn't have sagging shoulders or a furrowed brow; he's got a big ole grin! He says, "This joy of mine is now complete" (John 3:29).[13]

The only way John could have joy in a time of emptied-cup decrease is by refusing to be stuck in selfie mode. John pictured himself not as a main character but off to the side in a story that's all about Jesus. If we want to have joy in times of emptied-cup decrease, this strategy works well for us, too, though it's not intuitive or popular.

In our world, it almost seems wrong to put ourselves off to one side, especially when we're feeling inadequate or "less than." In those empty-cup moments when our self-worth needs buoying, the most intuitive response is to flip our lens back to selfie mode and add captions like "loved" and "priceless" and "I am enough." And, while every single one of those is true because of Jesus, **trying to solve the problem of self-focus with more self-focus isn't helping. It's making things worse.** We find freedom, joy, and confidence when we—like John—put the focus back on *Jesus*.

To illustrate this contrast, let's consider what John's wedding attendant imagery looks like when we flip it to selfie mode.

A ME-FOCUSED ATTENDANT

There's a wedding. The ceremony has begun. Just as the groom begins speaking his vows, one of the attendants clears her throat loudly and begins waving her arm a bit. When she succeeds in interrupting and drawing everyone's attention to herself, she says, "Hi, everyone! I've been trying to get your attention all morning. I wanted to let y'all know that my shop's grand opening is *today*! It's on Broad and Main, just around the corner. I'm hoping everyone will have a chance to stop in. We're doing giveaways! And we have such nice pieces. I'm going to head over now, actually, okay? So please come!"

She excuses herself, walks briskly to her shop, and then spends the whole day pacing and fretting because no one comes. As the bell on the door refuses to jingle, the old feelings of inadequacy and low self-worth rise up. She begins worrying about what everyone thinks. Is she accepted? Does she have value? She pulls up her pinned memes to remind herself of the truth. She is special. She is enough. God created her uniquely, with special design.

Again, all of those things are absolutely true. But isn't it also true that her self-focus is skewed? Friends, we *are* special. We *do* have such great value and worth. But we are not the main character in the story! And if we're trying to be, it's no wonder that we struggle with inadequacy and low self-worth. We're trying to fill a role that wasn't meant for us. We're trying to rival *Jesus*.

THE GREATEST STORY

The whole world tells a story about our Creator. Each chapter of earth's history chronicles a new detailed account of God. Yes, you and I are tucked into tiny paragraphs. Our lives are important and seen. But every line of the story showcases his glory, not ours.

The Bible—filled with the words of God—offers a framework for our tiny paragraphs. It's a story about a loving Father pursuing his children and paying their ransom, about a spotless Lamb dying to take away the sins of the world, about a groom giving his life for his bride, about a conquering lion who swallows up death. But here's what the story is not about: you and me trying to prove our measure-up worth.

Each occasion to insist on my own importance is also an opportunity to exalt Christ. Those times that I feel marginalized, belittled, or replaced are often my *best* opportunities to exalt Christ. By saying, with a big ole grin on my face, "He must increase, but I must decrease," I make much of King Jesus.

≈ Sometimes our exaggerated sense of inadequacy is a sign that we're stuck in selfie mode. How have you found this statement to be true: "Trying to solve the problem of self-focus with more self-focus isn't helping"?

≈ Read John 3:31. List the comparisons John makes between Jesus and everyone else. Draw a stick person diagram of the truth from this verse.

≈ How are you feeling marginalized or unappreciated? How is your time of "decrease" providing an opportunity to exalt Christ and make much of him?

≈ List several practical ways to say, "Jesus must increase and I must decrease," with your life.

For Meditation: John 3:30

He must increase, but I must decrease.

When I want to be lifted up more than I want Jesus to be lifted up, I have made him my rival. My freedom comes from living me-free. *Lord, help me to find joy by placing myself off to the side in a story that's all about you.*

Lesson 5: A Place to Belong
Read 1 Corinthians 12:1–26

WHEN KATE WAS in third grade, her teacher called her house. She wanted to offer Kate's mom some guidance—not on reading or math but on Kate's hair. Kate is bi-racial and has beautiful African American hair. But her natural afro wasn't in style at the time, and the kids were picking on her. The situation was bad enough for the teacher to notice and call Kate's Caucasian mother, who was grateful for some hair styling advice from a woman who was black herself.

Kate had always known she was different, but her third-grade class had now decided "different" meant ugly. And like a real-life ugly duckling, Kate decided they were right.

Our enemy loves to use differences to cultivate our attitudes of superiority and inferiority. He doesn't care whether we compare and emerge with an inflated ego (like third graders deciding someone God created was ugly) or a sense of deflated worth (like a third-grade girl deciding her class was right). Either way, our enemy wins by dividing us.

The message "You don't belong. You are beneath me," is rarely spoken but often communicated—among both children and adults. The "superior" one stiffly turns her back and walks away, then the "inferior" one responds the same. After being treated like *that*, why would she stick around for more? As we look down our noses, turn our backs, retreat to our corners, and put up thicker comparison walls, guess who's throwing his head back and cackling with glee? Never Jesus; always Satan.

Our disgust toward each other—I call it the "Disgust Factor"—easily widens the divisions between us. In the world, it feels natural to get into our little groups and decide who is disgusting and why they don't belong. But in the kingdom of heaven, everyone belongs. **In God's family, everyone is celebrated—not because we are all the same, but precisely because we are *different*.** Our goal is to create unity, not uniformity. If everyone were uniform, why would we need unity?

A Diverse Unity

The church is arguably the most diverse group of people in the world. Our membership includes every nationality, race, income bracket, competency level, and age group from every century since the time of Christ. One day our God will receive the worship of a people made up of every tribe and tongue, gathered around his throne (Rev. 7:9–12). And to help draw this diverse group together in unity, God makes us . . . wait for it . . . different. Not the *same*, since that would make us uniform. To give us unity, God makes us *different*.

In his amazing wisdom, God tucks unique gifts into our Comparison Girl hands and hearts that are meant for each other. He gives one person more of this and another more of that. He purposefully mismatches us so that we'll be drawn together—out from behind our comparison walls. So not only are we an eclectic-*looking* group, we bring diverse gifts, abilities, passions, and callings to the table—each fueled by the same unifying Holy Spirit.

Smorgasbord Style

When my kids were young, my husband would take them to the store on Super Bowl Sunday and let them each pick out two of their favorite snacks or treats. They always came back with big smiles, ready to build a smorgasbord of junk food on the kitchen counter. They never got jealous of each other's snacks. They never said, "What? Dad got you M&M's?" Nor did they brag about their snacks, saying, "Dad got licorice for me, not you." They knew that the M&M's, licorice, and everything else was meant to be shared. And so it is with the gifts given to the members of the church.

Perhaps it's because our Father doesn't allow us to *select* our gifts that we become grumpy Comparison Girls in the church. But since our gifts are meant to be shared smorgasbord style, shouldn't we be rejoicing in our differences? If ten bags of the same potato chips are lined up on the counter, we're likely to each grab our own bag and scatter. But when each person brings something unique to the table, we're naturally drawn together.

In the following verses, put a group of dots over words that represent differences or variety. (You can make your dots different colors or shapes if you'd like.) Then put a "1" above words that indicate "one" or "sameness."

> Now there are varieties of gifts but the same Spirit; and there are varieties of service, but the same Lord; and there are varieties of activities, but it is the same God who empowers them all in everyone. To each is given the manifestation of the Spirit for the common good. . . . All these are empowered by one and the same Spirit, who apportions to each one individually as he wills. For just as the body is one and has many members, and all the members of the body, through many, are one body, so it is with Christ. For in one Spirit we were all baptized into one body—Jews or Greeks, slaves or free—and all were made to drink of one Spirit. (1 Cor. 12:4–7, 11–14)

Exchanging Gifts

Perhaps you've been told, "Just stop comparing." Yet since this passage goes to great lengths to point out our differences, it makes sense that God wants us *to* compare—only in an upside-down way. In the world, we compare by measuring ourselves against each other. We focus on the lines and attach value statements to our notable differences. But in the church, we use Jesus's upside-down way of comparison. We focus on the spout.

When my measuring cup is tipped, my differences take on new purpose. Rather than prompting me to puff up or deflate with self-focus, my differences suddenly offer me a unique, spout-focused way to serve others. As I compare myself with someone else, I say, "How can I provide something she needs?" Or, "How will God use her gifts to help me grow?" Rather than measuring from behind our comparison walls, we're gathering together and exchanging gifts—which causes two things to begin happening.

First, we experience God in new ways. Even right now, as I use my gifts to write and encourage you, sometimes it almost feels like God finishes my sentences. I look back at a section I've written and think, "That is better than I could've done." I know my inadequacies well and am amazed by God's guiding power, filling me. As you and I pour ourselves out to serve God and others, he supernaturally replenishes our cups. In wrung-out moments, when we are convinced we have nothing to give yet tip our cups over anyway, God's Spirit fills and empowers us in exciting ways.

Second, as we all tip our cups simultaneously—each pouring out what we've been given and receiving the gifts of the others—a unique unity forms. Nobody is trying to prove that they have more or are more. With our cups tipped, the lines don't matter, so our insecurities, self-consciousness, pride, and self-sufficiency melt away. As we share what we're given, we have new purpose: we give each other a place to belong.

You're Indispensable

I'm sure you've noticed, however, that the church is not always the perfect display of unity. It's because, unfortunately, the very differences meant to unite us often divide us. This happens when we play the Comparison Game: Church Edition. After highlighting the differences meant to unify us, Paul spends the rest of 1 Corinthians 12 warning against measure-up comparison, using an analogy of one body with many diverse body parts.

First we hear from the body parts that compare and feel inferior. The foot feels inferior to the hand. The ear feels inferior to the eye. They say, "I'm obviously not needed here." But what good is a detached foot or eye? Of *course* these members are needed.

Next we hear from body parts that compare and feel superior. The eye sees no need for the hand. The head sees no need for the feet. They say, "Obviously we don't need you here." But a body losing a hand or foot would be tragic. Of *course* these body parts are needed. They're indispensable.

When my pastor, Jeff Manion, preached on this passage recently, he told us about his granddaughters Hazel and Cooper, who were born just weeks apart. Because of Hazel's Down syndrome, she has experienced developmental delays. So Cooper learned to crawl before Hazel did. Cooper learned to walk before Hazel did. Cooper learned to talk before Hazel did.

In fact, at three years old Hazel is still struggling with speech, but she's learned sign language. So the first thing Hazel does when Grandma picks her up from preschool is to make the sign for *Grandpa*, asking where Jeff is—which he loves.

He said, "She's got speech therapy twice a week and physical therapy one day a week. This is a hassle, but *she's* not a hassle." With deep emotion, he continued, "Our family . . . we need her. As she is. Without her, our family wouldn't be our family. We need her to be *us*."[14]

In the way that Hazel is celebrated in her family, each one of us is celebrated in the family of God. We're all needed. We all matter. We all bring something that only we can bring.

As a Comparison Girl, maybe you don't feel indispensable at your church. Or you *do* feel indispensable, yet you think others aren't. Both of these are false conclusions of measure-up comparison. Here's what God wants you to know: each part of the body is indispensable. And he has strategically arranged his church so that your differences and others' differences give each person—everyone—a place to belong.

The One Who Has More

God wants all of us to cultivate unity, but Paul gives special instructions to a particular group of us. He says that the more "presentable" parts (think up-front types) are to bestow honor on the "unpresentable" parts (think behind-the-scenes types). And guess what? In order to decide which is which, you have to compare.

Are you particularly gifted, strong, relied upon, or easily recognized? Is it obvious to others that God has filled your measuring cup with gifts that are useful for building up the church?[15] It's not wrong to be more gifted any more than it's wrong to be less gifted. Gifts are gifts. We don't choose them or bestow them upon ourselves, and our gifts don't add to our value. Let me say that again. Your high level of giftedness does not add to your value. Yet when God fills your measuring cup fuller, he does give you an extra responsibility. It's the secret sauce of unity in the church. Are you ready? If you answered yes, here's your instruction. You're to identify those who are at risk of being marginalized or overlooked and lift them up (1 Cor. 12:23).

If you are a particularly gifted woman, your humility has such influence. When you tip your measuring cup over and lift up those who feel small by making *yourself* small, you represent Jesus so well—for isn't this what he did? Lifting others up doesn't mean you deny what's in your cup or pretend your gifts aren't there. Nor do you deny your dignity or worth. Jesus did none of these things when he humbled himself and became a man. His greatness was unsurpassed, and yet his humility made him greater still (Phil. 2:8–9). And when you—like Jesus—count others more significant than yourself (Phil. 2:3), you, too, are enhanced by humility.

Perhaps you've noticed this phenomenon in others. When a notably gifted woman lifts others up rather than comparing down or snubbing, doesn't your appreciation for her grow? As John Dickson points out in his book *Humilitas*, "Humility makes the great even greater."[16] And 1 Corinthians 12, verses 23 and 25, points out another benefit: "On those parts of the body that we think less honorable we bestow the greater honor . . . that there may be no division in the body." When honorable people give honor away, unity tightens. And it's the sort of unity Satan can't throw a wrench into.

GREATER HONOR

My family attends a large multicampus church with a production team that oversees our worship services. So when my daughter, at age seventeen, was invited to play keyboard for the worship team, she was both thrilled and intimidated.

Lindsay remembers her hands trembling on the keys the first time she helped lead worship from the platform. She bobbed her head and visibly counted *one, two, three, four* while playing. Bless her heart. She was trying so hard to do well.

But you know what really blesses *my* heart? Two adults Lindsay shared the platform with. Ash once toured as a professional singer and has a stunningly beautiful voice. Joel is an outstanding electric guitarist. Both of them serve on our church's worship staff, and both went out of their way to encourage and affirm Lindsay.

As an out-of-state college student, Lindsay continues to serve on the worship team when she's home because it's both a way to serve and a way to belong. Last summer, backstage during a rehearsal, she overheard Ash and Joel reminding each other to give the new drummer—a high school student—extra encouragement. *That's how they probably talked about me,* Lindsay thought with a smile.

It's obvious that Joel and Ash deserve more honor. But instead of rolling their eyes when a teen expresses interest in leading worship, or critically drawing attention to Lindsay's awkward mistakes, Joel and Ash give "greater honor" to the less experienced musicians who play beside them. In doing so, these "greats" become greater still as they cultivate unity and belonging.

Friends, we are all so different. We are black and white. We are rich and poor. We are blue collar and white collar. We are young and old. We are married and single. We are women and men. We are the church.

Satan wants to tear us apart with the same vicious brutality used to tear at Christ's body. And with what does our enemy attack? He weaponizes the very differences meant to unite us. With self-focus flooding our hearts, we glance sideways and notice differences, then conclude, "They obviously don't need me" or, "I obviously don't need them." But this is not something Jesus would ever say. Our unifying

King Jesus—the head of the body—calls out with wisdom from above, inviting us to compare in his upside-down way and say, "They need me here. Who can I serve?"

Are you a follower of Jesus? Then you were designed to be part of his church, which is marked by diversity. God strategically arranged things so that one particular item is missing on the smorgasbord—the one he placed in your hands. How will you humble yourself to both give and receive from others? By this, you cultivate unity and create a place where everyone belongs.

≈ Tell about a time you experienced a sense of belonging with other Christians. How were your unique gifts validated and received? How did you validate and receive the gifts of others?

≈ Write or print out 1 Corinthians 12:12–26 and add a "+"above any examples of superiority and a "-" above any examples of inferiority. Circle any words or phrases that stress unity.

≈ In that same passage, underline any of the quotes that sound most like something you would say or think. How has this sort of thinking caused you to pull away from other Christians? Which attitude or reaction is God asking you to change?

≈ Make a list of the ways God has filled your measuring cup with unique gifts, abilities, and resources.[17] How is he asking you to serve others with what you have? How might this forge unity?

For Meditation: 1 Corinthians 12:24–25

> But God has so composed the body, giving greater honor to the part that lacked it, that there may be no division in the body, but that the members may have the same care for one another.

God created our differences to unite us; our enemy uses our differences to drive us apart. Unity, not uniformity, is the goal. *Lord, I want to bring my gifts to the table and receive others' gifts—so that we all give each other purpose and a place to belong.*

Chapter Two

Comparing Your Sin and Mine

ONE DAY WHEN our son Cade was about three, my husband said, "Shannon, we've got to be consistent with disciplining Cade for talking back. Should he sit in the corner for five minutes?" I agreed, and while Cade was in his little chair facing the corner, his older brother slipped over to share an idea with me.

In a lowered voice, he said, "Mom, I've been thinking. Cade has some things he really needs to work on. So maybe the four of us—you, Dad, Lindsay, and me—could have a meeting and talk about how to help Cade with his sin. You know . . . we could maybe have snacks and share ideas?"

It made me laugh to picture what six-year-old Cole had in mind. Would Cade be over in the corner while this meeting took place? Would he be able to smell the snacks and overhear our creative sin-correcting ideas?

As Comparison Girls, we have a tendency to magnify other people's sins and minimize our own. It feels good to point at the obvious offender over there in the corner. It makes us want to circle up at the judge's bench to share stories and have snacks. But Jesus says that the best story is told by the individual who knows she belongs in the corner and who cries out, "God, forgive me, the sinner!" For she is the one who gets to meet the lifter of her head (Ps. 3:3).

Lesson 1: Sideways Disgust
Read Luke 18:9–14

KENDALL AND I were sitting cross-legged over in the corner of the room. It was Vacation Bible School at our church, and she had responded when I shared the gospel from the platform. "Kendall, are you feeling convicted about your sin?" I asked. I always begin this way when talking to children about salvation, because they can't understand the good news unless they understand the bad news. But Kendall didn't understand either.

"Oh, I don't sin," she said.

So I read a passage from the New Testament which lists a bunch of sins and asked, "Have you ever done any of these?" She hadn't. So then I read Romans 3:23, "For all have sinned and fall short of the glory of God." I emphasized the word *all*. Kendall listened politely then said she was ready to go back to her group. When we got there, her small group leader excitedly asked Kendall if she had anything to share. She did.

Kendall said, "*All* of you have sinned." With the word *all*, she dramatically swept her finger across the group. Then for emphasis, she leaned forward a bit more and repeated her finger sweep, saying, "*All* of you." Kendall had been reluctant to admit her own sin, but now she seemed almost gratified at the opportunity to let the rest of her group know about theirs.

Now before we go snicker behind our hands, let's consider how, to some degree, Kendall represents us all.

TWO BAD GUYS

In our study today, Jesus will tell a parable to some religious leaders "who trusted in themselves that they were righteous, and treated others with contempt" (Luke 18:9). These leaders thought sin was everyone else's problem, not theirs. Have you noticed how self-righteousness and contempt often pair up in our hearts? When we measure our goodness against other people's badness, we naturally look down on them with disgust. So Jesus tells a story about a Pharisee doing just that.

"Two men went up into the temple to pray, one a Pharisee and the other a tax collector" (Luke 18:10). When you and I hear Jesus set up this story, we immediately assume the Pharisee is the bad guy. Why? Because that's what every Sunday school teacher, preacher, and Bible study leader has been telling us our whole lives. But Jewish people assumed the Pharisee was the *good* guy. Why? Because that's what *they* had been told their whole lives.

Pharisees were the ones who studied, interpreted, and taught the law of God which governed Israel. Everyone, especially fellow religious leaders, thought of them as elevated and superior. So as Jesus begins a story about a Pharisee and a tax collector, his audience is thinking, "Good guy, bad guy." In reality, they're *both* bad guys, and that is Jesus's point.

One more cultural note. When Jesus mentions entering the temple, you and I might picture two men walking into a church to pray privately, but Middle Easterners would have assumed these men were attending the morning or evening time of corporate prayer.[1] So in your mind, picture the Pharisee among other worshipers gathered at the altar, yet standing at a distance—not wanting to brush up against someone and be made unclean.[2]

Knowing there were other people around makes a difference when we hear the Pharisee's prayer, which he uses to distance himself even further: "God, I thank you that I am not like other men, extortioners, unjust, adulterers, or even like this tax collector" (Luke 18:11). This Pharisee may have walked in next to a tax collector, but spiritually they are miles apart, and he wants everyone to know it.

The Problem with Self-Righteousness

Now, the tax collector was the more obvious bad guy in the story. Tax collectors collected taxes not for Israel but for Rome—who had occupied their land for almost a hundred years.[3] Rome's taxes were like a ball and chain, forever keeping the Jews from prosperity. Then the tax collectors made themselves rich by adding their own heavy fees. The Jews looked at tax collectors in the same way I might look at a neighbor who gets rich off the pornography, trafficking, or drug industries . . . with extreme disgust.

Notice how the Pharisee puts the tax collector in another category. He doesn't thank God for keeping him from the greed of tax collecting. Betray his country? He would *never*! He *couldn't*. Instead he thanks God that he's not *like* the tax collector; he's not the *type* of person who would do such a thing—and he assumes that God agrees. The Pharisee fancies himself in a huddle with God, saying, "Can you believe that guy?" while God shakes his head, saying, "I know. He's so awful." But the Pharisee has it all wrong.

God's law, which the Pharisee knew frontward and backward, was not given so that we could differentiate and elevate ourselves. It was meant to show us each our finger-sweeping shared condition. *All* of us have sinned.

The problem with self-righteousness is that it's based on self, making it very skewed. The Pharisee saw himself as righteous because of all the things he did and didn't do—which he lists out tidily in his prayer. He's comparing *down* with the tax collector, but he's missed the point entirely. What he really needs to do is compare *up* to God.

If we could see how great and pure and holy God is, we would never elevate ourselves in his presence. Instead of gossiping to God about some other sinner, we would know we need to talk to him about ourselves.

The Sin of Disgust

Picture yourself walking into church. You notice another woman walking toward the door who doesn't "belong" in church. Maybe you know some details about this particular woman or she's a type of woman you'd have difficulty sitting next to.

Are you having trouble picturing that woman? Maybe you welcome everyone, assume the best, and always show kindness and grace. Then, consider this. How do you feel about the ones who *don't* show kindness and grace? That church lady who rolls her eyes in disgust, unwilling to sit next to the "sinner." If your reaction is, "That bigot! I would never treat people the way *she* does," are you not also comparing down with disgust?

Here's the problem. **We Comparison Girls tend to minimize our own sin of looking down on sinful people.** It's one of those "respectable sins" that even the godliest women among us—the ones who lead Bible studies and make food for funerals and pray daily over their grandchildren—do on a regular basis. And we feel comfortable following their lead.

"I would *never*," we say, sweeping a finger of disgust over someone's sin. But in doing so, we fail to see our contempt as sin. Each eye-roll, horrified gasp, or look of disgust cast toward others is offensive to God, their Maker.

THE OPPOSITE OF LOVE

In his book *Christians in the Age of Outrage*, Ed Stetzer argues that the opposite of love is not hate but disgust.[4] Comparing down in self-righteous disgust makes love impossible. We involuntarily recoil, like the Pharisee from the tax collector. Or like Wendy from her friend.

Wendy was shocked when her dear friend confessed to getting Botox. *How vain!* Wendy thought. *I'm glad I don't do that. Everything I admire about her beauty is fake.* But then Wendy began to worry that their friend group might be wondering why *she* didn't get Botox. The thought made her self-conscious, so she secretly researched Botox pricing. Again, Wendy was shocked. She thought, *Geesh, it must be nice to be able to afford that.*

Over time, Wendy realized that her inward disgust was causing her to withdraw. She needed to humble herself and let her friend work out the matter of Botox and its affordability with God. It was only when Wendy stopped comparing down with disgust that her pure love for her friend returned.

Jesus wants us to love others the way he did. Not in a "love the sinner, hate the sin" sort of way but—as Stetzer puts it—in a "love the sinner, as I have been loved" way.[5] God has only assigned me one person's sin to deal with: my own. Everyone else I'm called to love.

THE DISGUST FACTOR CHALLENGE

As a Comparison Girl, I confess that, like Wendy, I've grown far too comfortable with my own disgust. I'm disgusted with unfaithful spouses. I'm disgusted with dirty politicians. I'm disgusted with the woman in the express checkout who has more than twenty items. *I would never*, I think to myself. But how quickly my disgust turns me into a proud, bitter, critical, condescending woman—exactly the type I never wanted to become.

I've noticed that when I look down on someone in disgust, I'm usually doing so from a self-elevated position. So to help root out my inward disgust (which is probably also more outward than I realize), I recently invited some friends to join me for a "Disgust Factor Challenge." For three weeks, we worked to expunge the disgust from our faces, words, and hearts. As my friends and I shared our progress, here are some situations that gave rise to our disgust:

- A coworker, once again, failed to do his job.
- A woman was sinfully dividing the church.
- A newly divorced friend was researching new ways to flirt.
- A family member in extreme debt booked a vacation.
- A friend shared a politically charged Facebook post.

Notice how our disgust was consistently triggered by a sin or bad habit that someone else needed to change. Yet as you know, disgust does not win friends or influence people. The moment I insert the "Disgust Factor," I only spark disgust in the other person and forfeit my influence. On the other hand, when I drop the disgust, the other person is far more open to listen.

I noticed this play out recently when I gave my teenage son some cleaning instructions. It was his fifth snow day in a row, and his chores would both save me time and give him something productive to do. But he rolled his eyes in resistance, which triggered an avalanche of disgust from me. "You've had *days* to do whatever you want. Why can't you just *help*? Do you really think that your video games are more important than my writing?" But then I remembered what I'm writing about.

I apologized to my son, then stepped back and repeated my message—this time minus the disgust. I did not contort my face. I did not point my finger. I did not raise my voice. I just said, "Honey, you've had a lot of snow days, and I have lots of work to do. Could you help me out by doing some cleaning?" The contrast in his response was remarkable. "Sure, Mom," he said and plugged in the vacuum cleaner.

When we approach other sinners with eye-rolling, finger-pointing disgust, we activate their defenses and push them away. Disgust only adds to our me-focused isolation.

AN INFINITE SHORTFALL

The Pharisee, praying loudly so that others in the temple could hear, expressed two things inextricably linked: One, he was righteous and the tax collector was sinful. And two, with his disgust the Pharisee revealed his own *un*righteousness. We've all sinned and fallen short of God's perfect standard. *All* of us. And that's really all we need to know. My "falling short" might be shorter than the next person's "falling short," but measuring the difference is not helpful. Rather than looking sideways at others to measure sin, I need to consider God's righteousness.

Because God is infinitely pure, my sin against him is proportionately infinite. I used to explain it to my kids this way. I'd say, "Suppose you hit your brother. That would be bad, right? But if you lost your temper and hit your principal, that would be worse, right? And if you punched the president of the United States, that would be worse yet. But what if you punched *God*?" The severity of an offense depends not only on what we've done but whom we've offended.

Because God's worth is infinite, our punishment for sin—even small sins—must be proportionately severe. When we stand before God, if he judged by merit, we would each be declared guilty—subject to a trillion-year-plus sentence. It would take eternity for justice to be served. How ludicrous, then, for one trillion-year felon to look at another trillion-year felon with disgust, saying, "I would *never.*" And how astonishing that God would look upon each with compassion over what we're going through and love this profoundly: "But God demonstrates his own love for us in this: While we were still sinners, Christ died for us" (Rom. 5:8 NIV).

One Went Home Justified

In the parable, both the Pharisee and tax collector were sinful, but only one knew it—and it showed. The tax collector pounded his chest and would not even lift his eyes to heaven as he begged God for mercy. In the original language, his prayer reads, "God, be merciful to me, the sinner!" He wasn't looking sideways at others; his eyes were downcast as he humbled himself before God. And he, not the other, went home justified.

The psalmist David sings of crying aloud to God in Psalm 3:3: "But you, O LORD are a shield about me, my glory, and the lifter of my head." Our God lifts the head of the one who lowers herself in remorse over sin, not the one who foolishly holds her head high, looking down her nose at other sinners.

Red-Letter Comparison: The person who exalts herself will be humbled, but the person who humbles herself will be exalted (see Luke 18:14).

Jesus closed the story with one of his red-letter comparisons: the person who exalts herself will be humbled, but the person who humbles herself will be exalted (see Luke 18:14). As I listen in, I hear Jesus inviting me to find myself in the story. Am I like the Pharisee, exalting myself and looking sideways with disgust? Or am I the tax collector, looking down with remorse and humble repentance? All of us have sinned, but only the humble encounter the "lifter of my head."

≈ Have you—like the Pharisee—put yourself in a different category from another sinner by expressing disgust? How is God asking you to make this right?

≈ By telling this story, what is Jesus's message to those who compare down with disgust?

≈ Read Romans 4:4–8. Take a sheet of paper and fold it down the middle. Now unfold it and draw a stick figure of yourself on one

half. Next, take a stack of sticky notes and list your most grievous sins. Cover your stick figure self with the sticky notes. On the
other half of the page, write "God" in the largest lettering possible, then draw arrows from each sin toward God—since he is the
one you've offended. Now draw a large cross between "you" and
"God." One by one, remove your sticky notes and shred them. In
the space above "you," write "Jesus's righteousness." Pray Romans
4:7–8 aloud.

≈ Read Romans 5:8–11. How did Jesus's death on the cross make a
way for you to be justified, or cleared of guilt? Who do you need to
share this good news with?

For Meditation: Romans 4:7–8 (NLT)

> Oh, what joy for those
>   whose disobedience is forgiven,
>   whose sins are put out of sight.
> Yes, what joy for those
>   whose record the LORD has cleared of sin.

When I measure my sin by looking sideways with disgust, I only feed
my self-righteous pride. Instead, I should look up. *God, be merciful to me—
the sinner. Thank you that Jesus made a way for my sin to be cleared.*

Lesson 2: An Empty Courtroom
Read Luke 18:9–14

WHEN JESUS CLOSED his parable by saying that the tax collector went home justified, there were probably some audible gasps. No doubt Jesus's audience expected the Pharisee to be the one exalted.

In your mind's eye, picture the Pharisee as he walks into the temple. Put a little bubble over his head that says, "I'm the good guy." And then put yourself in his sandals.

COURTROOM LANGUAGE

Jesus told this parable to "some who trusted in themselves that they were righteous, and treated others with contempt" (Luke 18:9). Last time, we talked about the problem of comparing down with contempt and disgust. This time we'll talk about trusting in ourselves to be righteous. We'll also turn the tables and talk about the despair we feel when our measuring cup is empty of righteousness and everybody knows it. Once again, there's a lot for us to learn.

Jesus closed the parable of the Pharisee and tax collector by telling us that one of the two men was "justified"—which is a courtroom word. It has "justice" at its root. To be justified is to be proven right, and in the story that's what the Pharisee is after. He may have been going to the temple to pray, but his words—reflecting his heart—made it sound like he was in court.

He begins by calling himself to the stand as a character witness, saying, "I am not like other men, extortioners, unjust, adulterers, or even like this tax collector" (Luke 18:11). Then he offers more physical evidence, saying, "I fast twice a week; I give tithes of all that I get" (Luke 18:12).

The Pharisee isn't really focusing on God as he prays in the temple. He's actually looking around at the other people to build his case. His efforts far exceed everyone else's, since fasting twice a week isn't required, nor is tithing on his purchases (which other people should've already tithed on).[6] Plus, these other people are sinning in ways that he *isn't*. Compared with them (and especially with that tax collector), he's a saint!

As the Pharisee presents his integrity, virtuousness, and faithfulness as a husband as evidence, he's making his closing statement: he's one of the good guys. But the fact that he's trying to build his case is exactly the problem. Nobody goes to court to argue that they're a bad guy. Everyone goes in to exonerate and exalt themselves. Yet "there is no one righteous, not even one" (Rom. 3:10 NIV).

COMPARISON GIRLS IN COURT

As Comparison Girls, we look sideways like the Pharisee, trying to prove that we're right, not wrong. We present evidence that we're good, not bad. We provide proof that we measure up. Tim Keller says, "What we are all looking for, is an *ultimate verdict* that we are important and valuable . . . And that means that every single day, we are on trial. Every day, we put ourselves back in the courtroom."[7]

Oh, how true this is for me. It's true when a friend challenges my choice of public school for my kids. Or a family member questions my motives as a working mom. Or my boss doubts my character by monitoring my spending. Whenever someone indicates that I am *wrong* in some way—that my cup is somehow lacking in righteousness—I have an instant surge of measure-up ambition. So what do I do? I haul open that heavy courtroom door and get back to work arguing my case.

I like to spend lots of time at the defense table facing an imaginary friend, relative, or even complete stranger over in the prosecutor's seat. I often put words into her mouth, based on what I assume she's thinking, and argue back, "Well, here's what you *don't* know . . ." Or, "Here's where you're making assumptions. Let me share *my* side." Like the Pharisee, I justify myself by pointing at others' flaws and presenting evidence in my favor.

Now, you should know that I don't hold these court sessions publicly. Actually, nobody knows I'm in there. On rare occasions I defend myself publicly, but I much prefer (like the Pharisee) to build my case in a setting where nobody can actually voice a rebuttal. And when I finish up, here's what I've noticed. The last thing I want to do is have lunch with the person I've just faced in court. So I avoid. I pull back. I let distance creep in. Like the Pharisee, I begin to enjoy the space around me.

I realize this probably sounds neurotic, but I wonder if you might be slightly neurotic too. Is there someone you've withdrawn from because you wonder what they *really* think? Do you go into the empty courtroom and defend yourself against the arguments that have or haven't been spoken? Do you fight for that final verdict, hoping to prove your value, importance, and worth?

GUILTY AS TRIED

Like the tax collector, we have a stack of evidence against us that is so thick and high, it reaches to the heavens. And one day we will stand before the Supreme Judge of the universe. If it were a fair trial, you and I would be eternally condemned by God. But this trial is *not* fair, because someone stepped forward to stand trial in our place.

> [Jesus] was handed over to die because of our sins, and
> he was raised to life to make us right with God. (Rom.
> 4:25 NLT)

Have you been made right with God? Like the tax collector, have you come to God in despair over your sin? Have you felt unworthy even to look up toward heaven—let alone look sideways to build your case? Have you come humbly, saying, "Have mercy on me, a sinner"?

If so, your verdict is in. The Judge has declared you "not guilty." Because of Jesus's sacrifice, justice has been served! This ruling should cause us to look at each other in amazed disbelief. Our trial is over! There is no condemnation. In Christ, we are *justified*. Hearing this, you and I should hug everyone in sight, with our mascara smearing, as we dance our way out of that courtroom.

That's what we should be doing. But many of us are acting like the trial is still going on.

Imagine this. What if Jesus continued his story and said that the tax collector, after returning home justified, returned to the temple day after day and began praying like the Pharisee—listing out all of the evidence for his righteousness? After such mercy, it doesn't seem fitting, does it? Yet this is exactly what I do when, after being made right with God, I head back into the courtroom to argue my case.

EVIDENCE LAID BARE

As a Comparison Girl who struggles with wanting to measure up, here is the question I'm learning to ask myself before I go back into the courtroom: Why does it matter so much if someone knows about my sin and imperfections? Hasn't the cross already exposed me? If I wanted people to think I was sinless, I certainly wouldn't mention that I'm a Christian, because Christians are the ones who say, "Jesus, I am wicked and I can't save myself!"[8]

Yes, others might point out the failings that I'd rather ignore. They might cast judgment because of how my kids are turning out or how my marriage is flawed. They might condemn my addictions to food or media, or my sinful habits of anger or worry. And when they do, my response must simply be, "Yes, but didn't you already know? I told you, I'm a Christian. Jesus died because of my sin. It's *that* bad."[9] And truly it is!

When Paul was facing the criticism of other people, he wrote, "It is a very small thing that I should be judged by you or by any human court. In fact, I do not even judge myself. . . . It is the Lord who judges me" (1 Cor. 4:3–4). The only courtroom I should be revisiting is the one where God has already ruled—and not to reopen my case, but rather as a pilgrim entering a sacred memorial.

The records are open, and I'm welcome to view them any time. All is laid bare before a holy God, offering evidence that proves two things. I am far more wicked than I ever realized and far more loved and valued by God than I ever imagined.[10] *What is the evidence of this love?* you ask. Exactly this: Jesus stood trial in my place. With every finger pointed in his face, he received my guilty verdict and drank up every bit of God's wrath. Why? Because he *loves* me. He *treasures* me. The evidence for this is shouted from Golgotha's hill and whispered from every page of Scripture. Jesus loves me, this I know.

Returning to Court

So then, what does it say about Christ's great love when I walk around like the Pharisee with a little bubble above my head that says, "I'm the good guy, and I'm going to prove it." What do I convey when I haul open that heavy courtroom door and get back to calling character witnesses, listing evidence, and working to be proven right? What do I communicate when I obsess over the judgment I see in others' eyes as they point to the lines? Or when I replay my heinous crimes and shrink back in shame?

By babbling on in my defense, I suggest that Jesus's blood was not sufficient. **By shrinking under another person's condemnation, I suggest that God's verdict was not final and that his ruling isn't highest.** By trying to cover my shame with evidence to the contrary, I suggest that my shame-lifter is not able. Yet not one of these suggestions is even remotely true.

Think of the red-letter comparison Jesus used to end his parable: "I tell you, this man [the tax collector] went down to his house justified, rather than the other. For everyone who exalts himself will be humbled, but the one who humbles himself will be exalted" (Luke 18:14).

The humble one is not the one arguing her case. The humble one goes down to her home quietly with tearstained wonder, amazed that she has been justified.

An Outside-the-Courtroom Conversation

It's a nice story—leaving the courtroom behind and walking home. Having my cup filled with Jesus's righteousness. But what about when somebody points to the lines that mark my sin and looks down at me the way the Pharisee looked down on the tax collector?

Living this already-justified life requires a lot of humility—especially because people will still point to the lines that mark our sin. They'll still look at me with contempt, the way the Pharisee looked at the tax collector. We've got to learn to have outside-the-courtroom conversations—like the one Nichole recently had with her friend Kelly.

Nichole and Kelly had been close friends. Zip-you-into-your-wedding-dress type friends. But several years back they had a sharp disagreement about something at church, and right then and there Nichole cut Kelly out of her life. They had not spoken since. Nichole hadn't even seen Kelly until recently, when at a sporting event with thousands of people, she looked up at the jumbo screen and saw Kelly's face. Her heart lurched. It was as if the Lord was pointing to Kelly in a big way—literally—and telling Nichole she needed to make things right.

For years Nichole had been wandering back into the courtroom. She would rehearse her arguments and accusations against Kelly, then defend herself against the words she assumed were in Kelly's mouth. But it was time to stop. "I think I'm going to reach out to Kelly after school is out," she confided in me the day after the jumbo-screen experience.

"But why wait?" I said. "It's March. Why put this off till June?"

A week later, I got a call from Nichole, whose voice was filled with emotion. The night before, she had been at a birthday party, and when she saw Kelly across the room, she went to her immediately. Before Nichole could even get any words out, Kelly grabbed her into a tight hug and would not let go. "Nichole, there is not a day that goes by that I don't think of you!" Kelly said. Nichole shared how God had convicted her of her hard-heartedness and lack of compassion over their disagreement. "I want to have you in my life again, Kelly!" she said.

God had allowed such sweet and immediate reconciliation, and Nichole was so thankful she hadn't waited any longer. She told me of their plans to get together soon, but she said, "I don't see any reason to hash things out." I one-hundred-percent agreed. Certainly there are times when deep wounds and ongoing offenses must be sorted out with difficult conversations involving repentance and forgiveness. But in this situation—a hard-hearted overreaction to a disagreement—why would they go back into that stuffy courtroom? Why rehash a few hurtful words—especially in the context of a close, decade-long friendship? God has redeemed both of these precious women by the blood of Jesus. They are free to have outside-the-courtroom conversations, full of love, joy, and reconciliation.

COURT ADJOURNED

Friends, court has been adjourned since Christ's resurrection. The verdict is in. Like the tax collector, you and I have been justified! So why are we wasting our time in court and withdrawing from treasured friends? Courtroom living is yet another trap of the comparison game. It distracts, divides, and causes us to withdraw from the unity and fellowship we need to thrive.

Stand with me for a moment, and gaze at the empty courtroom. Listen to the gavel fall and hear the verdict read. *Not guilty.* Feel your penalty and its condemnation lift. Let the peace of freedom and the joy of gratitude wash over you. You, my friend, are free to go.

≈ Read Romans 5:8–9, write down what Jesus has done for you, and record the final verdict. Does your heart respond (like the tax collector's) with tearstained wonder? Do you ever find yourself (like the Pharisee) rearguing your case?

≈ Is there someone you have been facing in "court"? Have you been putting words in their mouth? Have you been shrinking back from the condemnation (either real or imagined) you see in their eyes? How are you making their opinion of your sin matter more than God's? How is God leading you to have an outside-the-courtroom conversation?

≈ Write out 1 Corinthians 4:3–5. In verse 3, replace "you" with the name of the person(s) you have been feeling judged by. What does God show you about "staying out of the courtroom"?

≈ Read 2 Corinthians 10:12–18. How does verse 12 describe the Pharisee in Jesus's story? According to verse 18, who is commended?

Write out verse 17, then write a boast of what Jesus has done for you.

For Meditation: Romans 8:1

There is therefore now no condemnation for those who are in Christ Jesus.

Why do I keep re-entering the empty courtroom to argue my case? Why does it matter so much if someone knows about my sin? The verdict is in! Court is adjourned. *God, thank you that because of Jesus, I am justified.*

Lesson 3: God's Chair Is Off-Limits
Read Luke 7:36–50

WHEN OLIVIA WAS in tenth grade, her family moved to a new church, and a month later she attended a youth retreat. All was well until it was time to change for the canoe trip. When Olivia came out wearing a bikini, she immediately noticed the way the other girls—who were all wearing one-piece bathing suits—began glancing at her with disapproval.

This caught Olivia by surprise. Bikinis had never seemed wrong at her last church, but they obviously were here. She spent the day feeling self-conscious and uncomfortable, and worrying about fitting in. The first thing she said when she got home was, "Mom, we *have* to buy a one-piece swimsuit. I think two-pieces might be really *bad*."

These girls were, no doubt, trying to honor Jesus and their parents with their modesty, but I think they missed the point. Instead of dressing to please the Lord, they were using modesty like a measuring stick—with each inch of skin cause for more judgment. Yet were these girls in a position to judge Olivia's heart?

Olivia loves the Lord. She had not intended to be risqué or dishonoring. She never would have worn a bikini if she had known her new friends would be offended. Olivia—like many others who long to be welcomed in the church—was shamed because of a choice that her Bible does not speak directly against, over something she had never considered wrong.

I'm not saying moms should or shouldn't discourage teens from wearing bikinis. That's not the point. But I *am* saying that moms and daughters alike should be very careful about casting judgment and weighing heart motives, especially using our own list of rights and wrongs, because that's one thing that Jesus *did* explicitly warn against.

A SINFUL WOMAN

Today we're looking in on a dinner party that Jesus attended at the invitation of a Pharisee named Simon. If we were to spread out floor plans of a first-century home like Simon's, it would be common to find a walled courtyard area just inside the front door. In the same way that the pizza guy or a neighbor feels comfortable entering my front yard uninvited, people back then felt comfortable wandering into the courtyard area off the street.[11] So it wasn't weird that Simon had an uninvited woman very close to his open front door, but the next part was very weird. For she not only entered the public space, she came into the dining area where Jesus reclined on his side at the table.

This woman was known as a "sinful woman"—most likely a prostitute in her town.[12] When she learned that Jesus was having dinner at Simon's, she slipped in behind Jesus and began crying so hard that her tears made trickles through the dirt on his unwashed feet. Then she knelt and loosened her hair, using it to wipe his feet clean—kissing them repeatedly and anointing them with perfume.

This was all very uncustomary, and in lesson 4 we'll swing the spotlight to the woman and look at the details carefully. But for now let's zoom in on Simon as he watches this unexpected behavior unfold from his spot at the table: "He said to himself, 'If this man were a prophet, he would have known who and what sort of woman this is who is touching him, for she is a sinner'" (Luke 7:39).

JUDGE SIMON

Simon's thoughts revealed his version of the story unfolding around him. He was Judge Simon. And judges don't worry about defending themselves; their job is to convict and sentence others. Because of his superior morality and understanding as a Pharisee, Simon saw himself as being in a position to properly evaluate everything—especially this woman who had crept into his home. He knew who she was. He knew her type. And he could clearly see that she was defiling this so-called prophet with her ridiculous weeping and kissing. Did the man not know she was a sinner? A prostitute was kissing him, and he wasn't even stopping her! It was atrocious. Not only was Simon filled with disgust but he also started making judgments.

Before Simon could call for order in the court, there came another surprise. Jesus "answered" Simon's unspoken thought (Luke 7:40)—proving he was a prophet after all. Jesus used a story problem to reveal Simon's heart:

> If a creditor forgave two people their debts, one large
> and one small, which debtor would love him more?

Simon answered, "The one, I suppose, for whom he cancelled the larger debt" (Luke 7:43). Jesus then used this response to recast the *real* story unfolding at Simon's table. Jesus was not a fake prophet who was being defiled by a wretched woman. Jesus was a *real* prophet being honored by a woman whose great love was in response to great canceled debt. Jesus and the woman weren't the ones with mistaken judgment; Judge Simon was.

Simon's error is a textbook illustration of Jesus's teaching: "Judge not, that you be not judged" (Matt. 7:1). While our disgust is usually a gut reaction to something that seems wrong, our judgment is often calculated and precise, based on a careful examination of God's law. Disgust looks sideways at others and says, "I would *never* . . ." Judgment slides into God's seat and bangs the gavel, saying, "She should have never . . ."

Sometimes we Comparison Girls who know a lot about right and wrong assume that we're more qualified to judge, detect sin, and hold others accountable. **But like Simon, when we climb into the judge's seat, we often position ourselves to not see clearly—especially ourselves.**

Different Sin

One day during Bible study, Heidi said, "Don't worry if you didn't finish your lesson. I'm a leader, and I didn't finish mine! It's winter. We've all had sick kids. We've had snow days. I think the main thing is that we're here, opening God's Word together today."

But Barb, her coleader and mentor, pulled Heidi aside afterward and reprimanded her. Since Barb had strongly advised the women to be in the Word daily, she felt Heidi had been divisive and had undermined her authority. "You have given our women permission to be lazy and neglect spiritual disciplines, both of which are sinful!" said Barb.

The words cut deeply. Heidi had intended to be encouraging, not divisive. It took months to recover from these wounds, and that spring when it was time to renew her leadership commitment, Heidi took a hard pass.

Even as I share that story with you, I have to remind myself not to become sharply critical of Barb. Think about this: Those who criticize critical people *are* critical people. It's easy to spot this sin in others; it's harder to spot it in ourselves.

My friend Cindy Bultema says, "Let's be careful not to judge others because they sin differently than we do." Oh, how I need that reminder. You too? Do you find it easier to criticize people who sin differently than you do? Lazy people? Late people? Bossy people? Rude people? Are you judgmental of those who are overweight or in debt or who let their children run wild?

Simon felt qualified to judge the sinful woman, yet he was sinful too. By comparing down in harsh criticism, he revealed his own pride—which Jesus called him out on. By judging, he had qualified himself to *be* judged.

COMPARISON BY JESUS

"Then turning toward the woman he said to Simon, 'Do you see this woman?'" (Luke 7:44). Note that Jesus was prompting a Pharisee to compare himself with a prostitute. Of course, Simon already *had* been comparing, but Jesus was telling him to compare in his new upside-down way, which puts a premium on humility.

Then Jesus detailed the contrast in the greeting he had received from Simon and the one he'd received from the woman. Hospitality is a big deal in the Middle East (and is still today), yet Simon had not even shown common courtesy. No water for Jesus's feet, no kiss, and no anointing with oil. Skipping these gestures would be like you or I, upon a dinner guest's arrival, failing to go to the door, say hello, and invite our guest inside. The Son of God—the most valuable being in the universe—had come to Simon's house for dinner, and Simon had rudely ignored him.

But not the woman. It was clear that she *did* understand who Jesus was. In very personal and extravagant humility, she cast aside all decorum and used her tears, hair, kisses, and perfume to honor the lowest part of him—his feet.[13]

The perfume that she used to anoint his feet was particularly significant. In those days it was common for a wealthy woman to wear a little vial made of alabaster (a soft white stone[14]), filled with perfume and hung on a string around her neck. For a prostitute, though this perfume would likely cost everything she had, it offered allurement that was necessary for her trade. In order to pour out the contents of her vial, the woman at Jesus's feet had to snap the flask's long, skinny neck.[15] In doing so, she broke her ties with her old life and turned to the new.[16]

Unlike Simon, this woman saw that Jesus was the treasure worth forfeiting everything to have (Matt. 13:44). As she pours out her offering at his feet, it's clear that she has lost her life to find it (Luke 9:24). She—forgiven and clean—will live forever and dance on streets of gold, worshipping and exalting Jesus!

This is a beautiful scene between a daughter of the kingdom and her new King. Yet Simon is looking down with judgment and disgust.

THE GAVEL IS NOT MINE

Through the eyes of Jesus, the woman was the exemplary one, not Simon. She was the one who went in peace, forgiven. Could the same be true of some of the people *we've* judged? There is coming a day when every sin will be judged. No motive will stay hidden, no secret will go undiscovered. All will be brought to light.

Those who have believed in Jesus and made him their king will not be judged but will pass from death to life (John 5:24). Because of Jesus, they will be permanently pardoned and welcomed to the kingdom where there is no shame (Rom. 8:1). But those who have rejected King Jesus will stand trial on their own. They will be cast from his kingdom permanently with a judgment more harsh and severe than anything you or I could ever muster (Luke 13:27–28).

As Comparison Girls, when we find it gratifying to look down on others' sin with disgust, we should know we're sitting in Jesus's seat (John 5:22). We're like a preschooler, sneaking into the highest court and climbing into the world Chief Justice's chair. The gavel is not ours and we don't belong. Our preschool judgments will be instantly dismissed the day Jesus—our righteous King and Judge—orders everyone out of his chair.

Can I talk to the Comparison Girls who have been around church for a while? The ones whose slates are the cleanest and whose eyebrows shoot up the fastest? Friends, God's chair is off-limits. We don't belong up there. Playing judge is not good for us, and it's destroying the ones who really need our love.

SILENT TREATMENT

When Ann's son was expelled from Grace Christian School, she was devastated. She knew the school had made the right decision; drugs were found in Jack's locker. *Again.* He was obviously outside of God's, and the school's, code of conduct. But Ann felt like she also had been expelled.

The other moms at GCS were Ann's closest friends. They had served together for years, running concession stands and doing school fundraisers. Just last week, there had been a flurry of texts about homecoming plans. But the texts had stopped short. Not one person—not even Ann's closest friends—reached out. Her phone just went silent.

Jack's friends also backed away, saying their parents thought it best if they take a break. It was hard enough that Jack would never play basketball again or walk in graduation with the kids he'd known since kindergarten. But that pain was compounded by the rejection and shame expressed by silent Christian friends who were happily carrying on without him.

One day, after Ann picked up Jack from his day treatment program, they returned home to find several of Jack's teammates in their kitchen. Jack's sister had invited them, along with some of her cheerleader friends, not knowing that Jack would be back so soon. It was painful enough to walk in and see them there—eating snacks, laughing, and talking about that night's game. But it was devastating when these boys—who up until two weeks ago had been Jack's best friends—ignored his presence after a quick glance and hello.

Ann understood the need for caution and parental protection. Yes, her son had sinned. And drugs are harmful. She knew that more than anyone. But this community was acting like sin was a disease that nobody else had, only Jack.

Friends, sin is a disease that we all share. It's terrible. It hurts everyone it touches. But you and I have found the *cure*! **We've met Jesus— the one who is not defiled by our sinfulness but instead reverses it and makes us clean.**

We shouldn't ignore others' sin. Jesus didn't do that. (Just ask Simon.) Nor should we act like sin is a disease that we alone haven't been infected with. Whether it's over bikinis, comments made in Bible study, or drugs found in lockers, here's what I need to remember: I don't belong in God's chair. When I try to climb up and put myself in his place, I hurt the very people who most need my love.

≈ Is there someone you have been judgmental or critical of because they sin differently than you do? How have your judging thoughts qualified you to *be* judged? How will you respond to make this right before the Lord?

≈ Read Luke 7:44–47. How did Jesus compare Simon with the woman? In what ways are you like Simon? In what ways are you like the woman?

≈ Read Romans 12:19–20 and 1 Corinthians 4:5. What instructions and warnings do these verses offer? What comfort do you find regarding the hurtful sins of others?

≈ Write Romans 14:10–12 in your journal. Get on your knees, close your eyes, and envision the person you're tempted to judge on her knees next to you before Jesus. Confess the ways that you *both* have sinned. Now confess your critical spirit to King Jesus.

For Meditation: Romans 14:10

Why do you pass judgment on your brother? Or you, why do you despise your brother? For we will all stand before the judgment seat of God.

When I play judge, I'm sitting in God's seat. *Lord, help me to humbly use good judgment but leave the judging to you.*

Lesson 4: Flipping My Ruler
Read Matthew 7:1–5 and Luke 7:36–50

I PULLED INTO a parking space, then got out and leaned over to examine the dent in my back fender. When my eyes met with the other driver's, I smiled with kind empathy. It was her fault; no need to rub it in.

"Do you need me as a witness?" asked a third woman. The other driver and I smiled at each other knowingly, then told the woman no; we were fine on our own.

As she walked away, the other driver said, "Well, I guess I'll need your contact and insurance information," In surprise, I said, "That's fine, but you're not thinking this was *my* fault, are you?" Then *she* looked surprised.

"I wasn't even moving," I said. "I was waiting for the car ahead of me when you backed into me." Our kind smiles vanished. "No, you backed into *me*!" she said. "I looked behind me and it was clear!" Both of our eyes darted to the witness who had now entered the store.

I drove away that day absolutely convinced that I had done no wrong. Yet I think the other driver did too—which is such a good picture of sin. From the driver's seat in life, it's easy to spot everyone else's wrong-doings. It's natural to lean down and carefully examine the dents they've left. But in Jesus's kingdom, things are unnatural and upside-down. As Comparison Girls who want to be free, we need to stop judging others' sin and start examining our own.

MEASURING SIN BY THE MILLIMETER

Before we head back to Simon's dinner party, I'd like you to listen in on some earlier teaching from Jesus, during the Sermon on the Mount—which I like to call his "Ribbon Cutting Sermon," since it's the first time he introduced the upside-down kingdom and invited everybody in.

In this sermon, Jesus taught on the measure-up problem of judging, and he inserted some humor, using a size comparison between specks and logs. It's comical to think of yourself not even noticing a log sticking out of your eye. But even more so when you're trying to lean in and help someone with their speck.

Specks are tiny. If you were trying to measure with a ruler, you'd use the millimeter side. Logs are large. To measure a log, you'd flip your ruler around to the inches side. Maybe you'd even measure by the foot. Those of us who are judgmental or critical of other people tend to lean in and measure by the millimeter, saying or thinking things like, *Can you believe she smirked when he said that?* and, *I cannot believe he forgot my name.*

But Jesus said that when we critically judge and express disgust, our arrogance is log-size. Since our pride should be measured by the foot, how hypocritical is it for us—in our pride—to turn to inspect others' flaws by the millimeter. Here again, Jesus is inviting us to compare but in an upside-down, flip-your-ruler way.

A FLIPPED RULER

Several years ago, my daughter had a summer job and was struggling with a particular coworker. Lindsay is conscientious and enjoys thoughtful conversation. Her coworker was just plain silly. So as Silly Girl was wasting time, telling goofy jokes about poop and farts, then throwing her head back to laugh, Lindsay was grinding her teeth with steam coming out of her ears. She said, "Mom, what can I do? I'm about to explode!"

So we talked about specks and logs. I said, "Try flipping your ruler," and that's exactly what Lindsay did. Whenever she was tempted to lean in and measure Silly Girl's flaws down to the minutia, she would think about the millimeter side of her ruler and tell herself, "It's such a small thing. Look how tiny it is! And look how big my arrogance is when I judge her. It's log-size." Lindsay said it made all the difference. She actually felt physically relieved when she put down her "ruler" and chose to share the planet—and even her work space—with a girl who told silly jokes.

This ruler-flipping exercise isn't just meant for situations when someone's offense is a small annoyance. At Simon's dinner party, Jesus invited Simon to flip his ruler when evaluating a woman with great sin.

A Story of Two Debtors

As a religious leader and host of this dinner party, Simon was busy counting every miniscule way this unclean, sinful woman was defiling Jesus with her slobber and kisses. But Jesus drew Simon's attention to her heart.

She must've heard Jesus preach somewhere previously, and she obviously had "ears to hear" his call to repentance, because here she was repenting. But Simon had a log in his eye, preventing him from seeing what the woman saw clearly. Jesus was the most honorable, distinguished, fall-on-your-face guest Simon had ever received to his home. He was the savior, coming to rescue sinners like Simon and pay their debt! But Simon was too busy measuring by the millimeter to notice. Again, that's what the millimeter side of our ruler does. It draws our attention to the minutia of everyone else's sin and blinds us to our own self-inflated arrogance.

It's interesting that the story Jesus used to correct Simon put him side by side with a prostitute. Today's version of the story might go: One person owed $5,000 and another owed $50,000 in credit card debt. Neither one had paid the minimum balance in months, and the debt collectors were calling daily. But then the bank president called to say, "Your debt is forgiven. You have a zero balance."

Which one would love the bank president more? The one with the bigger debt. The answer was obvious, but its lesson was not. Jesus was drawing Simon's attention to a bigger, grander story that he was about to completely miss, there with his ruler in hand.

God's detailed laws about defilement and purification were like the fine print on a credit card agreement. They were intended to let people know God's requirements and expectations. But God's Levitical fine print wasn't written so that people could measure their sin against someone else's. The Ten Commandments (among others) show us our *own* accumulating debt before *God*.

The woman saw this clearly. Her great love for Jesus was in proportion to the great forgiveness she had received. So when Jesus said, "Simon, do you see this woman?" he was telling Simon to lean back and flip his ruler. Rather than measuring her sin by the millimeter, Jesus saw her forgiveness-inspired love by the foot.

Am I a Forgiven Woman?

How the woman's heart must have leapt when Jesus noticed and called out her extravagant display of love. Everyone else only saw her past. Simon thought of her as "that type of woman" (Luke 7:39) and wondered why Jesus didn't know. But here's the amazing thing: Jesus *did* know!

Though fully aware of every detail from her past, Jesus saw her as *forgiven*. In his eyes, she was even an example to be lifted up. Because her debt was paid, she could go in peace. **Oh what joy for the Holiest One to excuse you from a room of judgment and send you off to live your life in forgiven peace!**

Friend, regardless of what our pasts look like, haven't we all been sinful women? I think that's the point of this story. Some of us, if we visualized our sin debt all stacked up on the kitchen table, would measure by the inch, or probably the foot—like the woman at Jesus's feet. In comparison to Simon's stack, hers *was* higher. But since every bit of her stack was forgiven, the taller stack was only cause for greater love.

That bears repeating. A greater sin stack, when forgiven, is cause for greater love. That's the beauty of the upside-down kingdom. Those of us who see ourselves as the lowliest and worst sinners actually have an advantage, since we have no cause for Simon-type pride. We only have cause for awestruck wonder at Jesus's sweet forgiveness, and this love for him is what causes us to become great women of God.

Comparison Girl, if you—like this woman—have come on your knees in repentance and have snapped the neck of the vial which chains you to your sinful past, then here is how Jesus sees you: You are *forgiven*. In a room full of arrogant, self-righteous men, Jesus would hold *you* up as the example. He sees you differently than they do. He receives your tears and your kisses, not as defilements but as love from a woman who is *clean*.

AM I A DISGUSTED SIMON?

There are times I see my stacked-by-the-foot sin with such clarity that I crumble to the floor in a puddle of gratitude because of Christ's forgiveness. But I admit that there are times I also revert back to playing disgusted log-in-his-eye Simon. I hold the millimeter side of my ruler up in nitpicky judgment, completely forgetting about my own stack of sin. Does anybody else waffle back and forth? Here's the good news: We can't play both characters in this scene simultaneously. I can't be both crying at the feet of Jesus and judging others with disgust. So when I find myself leaning in to measure the minutia of someone's sin, it's time to flip my ruler and consider the magnitude of my own.

Like Simon and the woman, we're all just side-by-side sinners who have great big debts that we could never pay.

COMING CLEAN

My friend Tracy is a pastor's wife who shared the following message on her church message board:

> Ladies, I have a confession to make. Often when I come to church, my eyes are fixed on me, not Jesus. The Holy Spirit has opened my eyes to see how Satan has infiltrated my heart, keeping me from loving God with all my heart and loving others as myself. Here are some of the concerns God has brought to my attention:
> 1. I look at others with a comparing eye, not a loving one.
> 2. I feel jealous of other people.
> 3. I worry about what people think of me.
> 4. I worry I'll say the wrong thing and someone will think less of me.
> 5. I worry about what I'm going to wear and what I look like.
> 6. I don't think anyone likes me.
> 7. I don't feel like I fit in anywhere.

8. I only feel safe when the people around me agree with me.
9. I say things that are divisive.
10. I complain and speak negatively about everything.
11. I am distracted during worship, thinking about everything but the One we're to worship.
12. I listen to the message with a critical ear.
13. I wish someone else (who needs it more than I do) was here to listen to the message.
14. I serve out of duty not love.

Tracy's confession list dislodged an avalanche of confessions from other women at her church and resulted in true community and connection. That's what humility does. It draws us together as forgiven side-by-side sinners, rather than at-a-distance Simons looking down in disgust.

Comparison Girl, do you look down on others' sin? Do you despair over your own? Let's be women who love our Jesus—the one who died to forgive every one of our stacked-to-the-ceiling offenses.

≈ Tell which character you have been playing lately—Disgusted Simon or the Forgiven Woman. Support your answer.

≈ Is God asking you to make a confession like Tracy did? How would this prevent you from being a Disgusted Simon? How might it invite others to celebrate forgiveness from sin?

≈ Read Matthew 7:1–5. In tiny print, list any speck-size sins of others that you have been recently bothered by. Now in large print, list any log-size sins of pride, arrogance, or a critical spirit that you see in yourself. How can you "flip your ruler" next time you start noticing specks?

≈ Read Psalm 32:1–5. Notice the two uses of the word *cover* in verse one and five. (In other translations, you will find the words *conceal* and *hide*.) What happens when we cover or uncover our sin before the Lord? Is God asking you to uncover something? Make a plan to respond.

For Meditation: Luke 7:48

And he said to her, "Your sins are forgiven."

Since every bit of my sin stack is forgiven, a taller stack is only cause for greater love. *Lord, when I want to measure others' speck-size sins by the millimeter, I will flip my ruler and repent of my log-size pride.*

Chapter Three
Comparing Wealth

WHEN OUR DAUGHTER Lindsay was about five, my husband was tucking her in one night and she said, "Daddy, did you really sell our van for a dollar?" Apparently, she had been listening in to the conversation with our friends that afternoon. We had given them our van, but to make the transaction legal, Ken had asked them to pay a dollar.

Lindsay said, "Daddy, I think you could've gotten two dollars for that van."

We love that story. She was using her kindergarten judgment to offer her daddy some "wise counsel." If you can sell something for two dollars, why would you sell it for one? This didn't align with her kindergarten sensibilities. But then generosity doesn't align with any of our world's measure-up sensibilities.

In our world's economy, greed makes far more sense no matter how old you are. It's intuitive to fill our measuring cups with security we can liquidate and wealth we can measure. But when this mindset keeps us from generosity, it's clear we're listening to the wisdom from below. Remember, this is the wisdom that takes your hand and says, "You should do what's good for *you*." Jesus wants us to have the wisdom from above, which says, "You should do what's good—not just for you but also for others."

Yes, we could've gotten two dollars for that van or maybe two thousand. But in the upside-down kingdom, the joy and the rewards of generous living can't be measured.

Lesson 1: Putting My Name Tag on the Table
Read Matthew 19:16–22 and Mark 10:17–22

BRIAN AND SARAH live comfortably in a beautiful home—which Brian realized was becoming part of his identity. Where he lived was becoming who he *was*. So Brian initiated a "decoupling" exercise and listed their home on Airbnb. He wanted to put some actual space between himself and his residence, which meant that Sarah, who was expecting their fifth child, had to distance *herself* from comfort. Yet Sarah had to smile at the lesson they were all learning as Brian told their kids, "This house doesn't really belong to us. The stuff inside isn't ours. It all belongs to God, and he wants us to learn how to share."

Some people say that their things don't define them; Brian and Sarah's family lived it. For most of the summer, they stayed with family while other people slept in the beds, sat on the furniture, and enjoyed the amenities of a house owned by God, not them.

The American dream, as most imagine it, is not the dream of living in a mansion on a deserted island. It's the dream of living in a home and having a lifestyle that others can see and admire. It's the quest to prove that we measure up, and our cars, houses, clothes, and boats provide the tangible evidence. But the more we have, the harder it is to stop focusing on the lines. This was the case for the rich young man in our story.

RICH MAN RUNNING

Back when Jesus was traveling the roads of Galilee, rich guys didn't run. It was undignified.[1] But on this particular day as Jesus was setting out, a rich guy came running to catch him before he left town. In urgency, the man collapsed on his knees at Jesus's feet asking, "What good deed must I do to have eternal life?" (Matt. 19:16)

Friends, this rarely happens. For someone to be astute enough to both set his mind on things above (Col. 3:2) and run to Jesus for answers is profound and wonderful. Yet Jesus's response is perplexing.

He tells this earnest young seeker to go first and give his money away, then return and be a follower. This seems backward to me. I want Jesus to respond the way *I* would, and tell the guy that eternal life belongs not to those who do good deeds, but to those who believe. I want to jump out from behind the bushes and point emphatically at Jesus while quoting, "For God so loved the world, that he gave his only Son, that whoever believes in him should not perish but have eternal life" (John 3:16).

Yet Jesus gave the rich young man these directions: first go decouple from money, then come follow me. Other times, Jesus told people to leave everything and follow him immediately. One man wasn't even permitted to go back for a funeral (Matt. 8:22). So what is this generosity pre-errand all about?

Sometimes **I think we've turned "follower of Jesus" into a metaphor when it should be literal.** For the twelve disciples, following was literal. They walked on their feet wherever Jesus went, leaving behind jobs, houses, and people. They had been fishermen and tax collectors; now they were followers. Following was their new identity. True, it was their *belief* about what was up ahead, not their good *deeds*, which turned them into followers. But for each of them, following involved cost. And if this rich guy was going to become disciple number thirteen, there would be cost for him as well.

PEELING OFF HIS NAME TAG

Jesus's instructions to the man to give away all his money and then return to be a follower presented a problem. The rich young man had come looking for eternal benefits, not a new identity. He was already a pretty good guy. Maybe he'd even been generous. And while he had expected a new assignment—maybe upping his tithe by two percent or funding Jesus's preaching ministry—giving away *all* he had was a bit much.

This assignment from Jesus would require him to put his "Rich Young Man" name tag on the table and pick up one that simply said, "Young Man." For all his young life, money had shaped this man's identity. His wealth defined him. It differentiated him. What he *had* was who he *was*. But Jesus was asking him to peel that identity away.

As a Comparison Girl, do you need others to know you have money? Do you drop mentions of your latest vacation or your upscale shopping habits into conversations? Do you have the urge to give a tour when someone enters your house? Or show them photos of your boat? Or maybe for you it's the opposite. Do you keep your thrift-store shopping a secret or try to park your car with the rusty side not showing? Do you prefer to meet up away from home so no one sees where you live? Of all of the measure-up name tags that Jesus asks us to put on the table, our financial status might be the hardest one to peel away.

Yet Jesus is not interested in just giving us the kingdom; he wants to turn us into kingdom people. Ones who don't insist on being known as "wealthy" or who aren't driven by "wanna-be-rich" priorities. If we try to follow Jesus with our money-superiority or money-inferiority dragging along behind us, we're still living in me-focused bondage. Becoming a Jesus follower involves going from me-first to me-free.

Yes, this is a gradual process down a long road, but if we aren't even ready to *start* the process, we probably aren't ready to become followers. I think that's why Jesus told the rich young man to give first, then follow—not the other way around. **Giving doesn't make us followers of Jesus, but followers do give because it's who we are.**

The Good of Wealth

Jesus told the young man, "You lack one thing: go, sell all that you have and give to the poor" (Mark 10:21). What did he lack? He lacked the experience of *lacking*. It's hard to empathize with needy people if your own life is immune to need.

Notice that Jesus didn't tell the man to light a match to his money or throw it off a cliff. He said to sell his possessions and give to the poor. This man had overabundance while others lived next door in scarcity. Jesus wanted him to *see* that. To compare not with his eye on the measure-up lines but rather with his focus on the spout. Just think of how he could help! Imagine how many needs he could meet.

Money is not evil. Wealth can be used for so much good. And God expects us to *enjoy* the things that he has richly provided (1 Tim. 6:17).

Our goal as followers is not to blindly rid ourselves of money so that we can be poor; our goal is to rid ourselves of any superiority that keeps us from *seeing* and *serving* the poor.

It was the exception, not the rule, for Jesus to ask the rich young man to give *everything* to the poor. (Otherwise the rich and poor would just keep trading places.) Yet giving out of surplus should be normative. Randy Alcorn writes, "[God] doesn't want us to have too much or too little (Prov. 30:8–9). When those with too much give to those with too little, two problems are solved. When they don't, two problems are perpetuated."[2] God puts scarcity and surplus in our side-by-side measuring cups, and he does so on purpose. The disparity in our bank accounts is meant to draw us together as unified givers and receivers—not divide us as Comparison Girls.

I once hosted an open house for a missionary friend raising support, and though I had waved my arms around on social media and sent dozens of invitations, only a few responded. I knew I couldn't judge since I've often politely ignored similar opportunities to give, but still, I was disappointed. However, during that rather empty open house something wonderful transpired. There were older people and younger. White collar and blue. Those with deep pockets and no pockets at all. Yet these differences melted away as givers and receivers gathered in my family room and enjoyed the warm glow of community. There was no superiority. No inferiority. Just lives and purposes and bank accounts overlapping with joy as we followed Jesus together.

Giving sparks me-free community. When we say no to ourselves and choose open-wallet generosity, we experience unexpected joy. The rich young man experienced the opposite. As he turned with slumped shoulders and walked sadly away, Jesus gave commentary on what was happening, saying, "Many who are first will be last, and the last first" (Matt. 19:30).

LAST IN LINE

Picture yourself walking into Starbucks and holding the door for several people, then getting in line last. The woman who's first to the counter orders, then opens her purse and realizes her wallet is missing. "Oh no," she says to the cashier. And that's when you reach forward with a five-dollar bill and a smile. Coffee calamity averted.

From your place in line, you saw her need and were able to help. But what if you had rushed in, gone first, and spent all you had? Putting yourself last allowed you to see a need and provide.

Those of us who have extra cash in our measuring cups often walk through life's doors assuming it's okay to go first. We don't think of ourselves as entitled or privileged. Every dollar in our wallets feels earned. And the constant "asks" feel intrusive. But our perspective is never going to change unless we position ourselves to see differently. Privilege never *feels* like privilege. Yet here's how to put ourselves at the end of the line: When we limit our spending, we have more to give.

There are endless back-of-the-line giving opportunities. Missions trips. An unemployed neighbor. A medical bill. The church offering plate. My contribution might be big enough to change lives, or it might be so small it hardly makes a dent; either way, giving changes me. It helps me put my name tag on the table and see myself and others differently. When I tip my measuring cup, my eyes turn from the now-irrelevant lines to the people—who are always relevant. Giving positions me to *see* others, rather than being absorbed with how they see me.

DREAMS THAT MONOPOLIZE

Bruce and Sue were busily pursuing their dreams.[3] They had just purchased a second home on Lake Michigan—a dream come true—when Rita, a woman from Russia, came to stay with them. For two weeks Rita tagged along while Sue made trips to plant flowers. Trips to meet with landscapers. Trips to shop for furniture. When the visit came to a close, Sue asked, "Will it be hard to go back to Russia?" Sue was envisioning trips to stand in line for rationed food rather than their trips out to the lake house. But Rita said, "Oh no, I never want to be like you Americans. You spend all your time taking care of your things."

Rita's words sank deeply into Sue's heart, and she realized it was true. She told Bruce, "I think maybe we've believed a lie. I'm not sure the

American dream is what God planned for us. Maybe he gave us all of this to share, not consume."

Around that same time, Bruce heard a retreat speaker say, "What God needs is people who are available to love others," but *available* did not describe their lifestyle. Like the rich young man, Jesus was asking them to peel off their "Wealthy Couple" name tags and lay down some of the dreams which had monopolized their lives—beginning with the lake house. It sold within two weeks, and Sue was surprised when she felt relief instead of grief. No more trips carting kids back and forth to town for their activities. No more extra bathrooms to keep clean. No more broken jet skis, or any jet skis at all.

For Bruce and Sue, selling the lake house was a "name tag" exercise that led to a new lifestyle. It was like choosing to get in line behind others. They positioned themselves to be available and created new margin—both in their checkbooks and in their calendars—to invest in people they might otherwise have never encountered. Over the past decades, Bruce and Sue have led small groups, served on boards, and led retreats. They've invited numerous people to live with them and have shared their vacation condo. They even moved to the inner city with nine college students to serve as mentors. With joy, they have poured themselves out.

The rich young man refused to put his name tag on the table. He made the devastatingly sad decision to turn away from Jesus, not his wealth. And here's what would be even more disastrously sad: If one of us were to read this young man's story and make the same choice to turn away from Jesus.

Is your identity wrapped up in your money? Have you made what you *have* into what you *are*? Perhaps—like me—you don't have a lake house to sell, but is there some dream (American or otherwise) that has monopolized your life? Some measure-up house, neighborhood, car, or boat that Jesus wants you to stop pursuing?

Friend, your generosity might not create much change in the situation, but it always changes you. When you use your money to put others first, you position yourself to see them—rather than being absorbed with how *they* see *you*.

≈ How has the desire for "living the dream" created a comparison trap for you and your loved ones?

≈ How does this story of the rich young man illustrate Matthew 6:24? In what ways do you feel trapped or enslaved by your wealth?

≈ Is your wealth part of your identity? Tell about a time that you were generous. How did this turn your eyes away from self-focus?

≈ Read 2 Corinthians 9:6–15, and imagine the rich young man (who would now be an old man) reading this letter from Paul. How might he respond—especially to verse 11? How would our culture respond? And how is God inviting you to respond?

For Meditation: Matthew 19:21

Sell what you possess and give to the poor . . . and come, follow me.

God puts scarcity and surplus in our side-by-side measuring cups, and he does so on purpose. Giving changes the way I see myself and other people. *Lord, I want to limit my spending and practice open-wallet generosity. I want to position myself to put others first so I can experience me-free community and joy.*

Lesson 2: Camels Are Big; Needles Are Small

Read Matthew 19:16–26 and Revelation 3:14–17

I LOVED OUR new home but hated the bare, furniture-less spots. The thing bothering me most was the deck with no patio furniture, but luckily our tax return had just come, so Ken and I walked to a nearby coffee shop to discuss our spending plans. Sitting in a booth, we began cheerfully listing our wishes onto paper napkins, but when I glanced over at Ken's napkin, I froze. Even upside down, I could read "Giving" along with a number that had lots of zeros.

Instantly, my fun turned to fury. I snatched my napkin, ripped it up, and stormed out of the coffee shop. My baffled husband eventually caught up, walking beside me as I pumped my arms in fury. "Ken, do you know it is *okay* to spend our *own money* once in a while?"[4]

That tax return was ours. We were entitled to it. And I wanted *patio furniture*! But my sickeningly generous husband was about to guilt me into giving instead.

For Ken, giving is exciting. He gives out of joy, not guilt. He is one of the people who has truly latched onto Jesus's principal of storing up treasure in heaven, and I am obviously not. In rational moments, I say I'm proud of how he leads our family with a clear, heaven-minded perspective. But in *this* moment I was shredding napkins and storming off in my defiant love of things.

What would our friends think? I couldn't imagine hosting the parties I was planning that summer in our new house with its furniture-less deck! I remembered the time my friend had commented on her sister's card table set up in her dining room, saying, "Can she not even afford furniture?" I loathed the idea of someone saying that about me.

Ken stayed quiet and let me walk off steam for a couple of blocks, and then he took my hand and said, "Honey, I never intended to make you feel guilty. I really just *wanted* to give. But we don't have to. Won't you please tell me what was on your list?" Well, nothing diffuses a wife's greed-tantrum like a compassionate husband. I melted into tears, ashamed of my behavior. We shared our napkin lists, and when we tallied everything up, amazingly there was enough to give generously *and* purchase every other item—including the patio set.

My fear of not getting what I wanted turned to instant regret. I had the feeling I had just failed a test. While it isn't wrong to use money that God provides to buy things that we enjoy, it is wrong to make measure-up demands and throw Comparison Girl tantrums—as if God answers to me instead of the other way around.

Skipping Commandments

When the rich young man came asking about eternal life, Jesus not only said to give his money to the poor (which we talked about last time), he also said this: "If you would enter life, keep the commandments" (Matt. 19:17). The Ten Commandments, that is. When the young man asked which ones, Jesus listed them out—except he skipped some.

For a Jew, reciting the Ten Commandments (Exod. 20:1–17) would be like us reciting the pledge to the flag. Skipping over parts would be noticeable. Interestingly, Jesus skipped over the ones about God and money. Perhaps it was because the young man had been skipping these three as well:

1. You shall have no other gods before me.
2. You shall not serve replacement gods.
10. You shall not covet.

I don't think of myself as a breaker of these commandments, yet my shredded napkin tells another story. That night as I pumped my arms in fury, I didn't really care what God thought about how we spent our tax return. I wanted to measure up in the eyes of my friends. I wanted my house to be like their houses, and their opinion mattered far more to me than God's. I loathed the idea of being looked down upon, so I was willing to use every dollar I could to lift myself up. I was determined to live by the lines and not let even one drop of generosity spill out.

Our money always tells the true story of how we see God and how we see ourselves. The rich young man at Jesus's feet was convinced that he was a Ten Commandments follower. It's who he was. It's what he did. But when Jesus asked the young man to put these commands about God and money into action, it was a watershed moment—as often is the case.

~~Blessed~~ Tested

I like to walk on a trail that cuts behind a particular row of houses, and recently I noticed the swimming pools. I think there was only one a few years back. Now there are four, side by side. We Comparison Girls have that effect on each other. When one gets a swimming pool, a new car, or a new pair of shoes, we all want to. We laugh at ourselves and make light of the way we glance over the fence, then open our shopping apps, but maybe the underlying motivation isn't so funny.

"When you're greedy, you don't know that you are," says Tim Keller.[5] Let's test that premise. Who's greedy? Raise your hand. Anybody? Nobody?

As women with more disposable income than any preceding generation, we've got to consider that greed might be more of a problem than we realize. Those of us who have excess money (that's me, and probably you) often think of ourselves as blessed by God. But what if we're really being *tested* by him? What if—as God pads our purses and bank accounts—he's asking, "Will you love me most? Will you worship me, not this money? Will you serve *me* with what you have, not yourself?"

These are the exact tests Jesus put to the rich young man. "Go sell all you have and give to the poor," he said (Mark 10:21). While God rarely asks us to give everything to other people, he always asks us to give everything to him.

Psalm 24:1 says, "The earth is the LORD's and everything in it" (NLT). There is not one dollar bill in our measuring cups that God doesn't own, and he asks us to live accordingly. It's not that God is against wealth. He often blesses us with abundance, and he loves our gratitude and delight over a new patio or swimming pool. But God *is* against us holding something behind our backs and saying he can't have it or we won't give it because of some greedy measure-up goal.

WIDE OPEN HANDS

God told Israel, "There need be no poor among you" (Deut. 15:4 NIV). Make it personal and fill in your town's name: *There need be no poor among you in* _____.

God doesn't put equal amounts in our measuring cups. He puts those with surplus and scarcity side by side, then says to the one with extra, "Open wide your hand to your brother, to the needy and to the poor, in your land" (Deut. 15:11). In obedience the giver opens her hand, saying, "It wasn't mine to begin with" and the receiver says, "God is providing through her gift." And they both learn to trust God in a way that they wouldn't if they each had just enough.

So what does it mean, then, when I clench my fist and refuse to give to my neighbor in need? Am I not robbing both my neighbor and God—who put extra in my pocket for her? God had put lots of extra in this young man's pockets, and now he was asking him to open his hand wide. *Very* wide. It was a test and an opportunity to trust and put God first. Extra money always is.

CAMELS ARE BIG

Sadly, the rich young man failed this test. He had come with such promising earnestness. He'd do anything to have eternal life. Anything! But when Jesus asked for his wealth, his joy was instantly converted to sorrow. Look at the reason: "He went away sad, because he had great wealth" (Matt. 19:22 NIV). Perhaps if he only had a little, giving wouldn't be such a challenge. But because he had so *much*, he hangs his head and walks away in dejected resignation and sadness.

And Jesus said, "It is easier for a camel to go through the eye of a needle than for a rich person to enter the kingdom of God" (Matt. 19:24). In other words, it's impossible.

This shocked the twelve disciples. They asked in astonishment, "Who then can be saved?" (Matt. 19:25). Keep in mind that the disciples lived before the cross. When they broke the Ten Commandments (or other laws), the only way to be saved from God's wrath was by bringing lambs, one after another, to the altar to be slaughtered by a priest. Rich people could buy all the lambs they wanted, so the disciples thought of them as having a huge advantage. If a rich person couldn't be saved, they wondered, who *could*?

Because we live after the cross, we understand that the Lamb of God, who offered himself up once for all, takes away the sin of the world and gives us eternal life as a free gift (John 1:29; Rom. 6:23; Heb. 7:27). By Jesus, we are saved; by money, we are deceived.

Listen to Jesus's letter to the wealthy Christians of Laodicea: "You say, I am rich, I have prospered, and I need nothing, not realizing that you are wretched, pitiable, poor, blind, and naked" (Rev. 3:17). This makes me wonder what kind of letter Jesus would write to my church. How about yours? The people I know—both Christian and not—who are prospering and don't need help paying the bills seem happy about it. They would never call themselves (as Jesus does) "pitiable," nor would I. But could it be that the wealthy people filling our wealthy churches are just as deceived to their own condition as the Laodiceans? And what are the chances that you and I are among them?

Since the disciples mistakenly thought this man's money offered him a salvation advantage, he must have thought so too. But not Jesus. Jesus called the man's money a camel-size *disadvantage*—with the potential of keeping him *out* of heaven.

From Jesus's perspective, this man was a pitiable beggar in threadbare clothes, looking longingly at heaven's gate. And Jesus was giving him the chance of a lifetime—to enter and be wealthy beyond measure for eternity. All he had to do was empty the extra in his pockets and give his money to the poor. But he couldn't do it, "for he had great possessions" (Matt. 19:22). Perhaps if he had only five bucks in his pocket, he would have been willing. But five million? It was too much to give away. So instead, he let eternal life with its eternal wealth slip away.

Remember that Jesus's first response to the rich man on his knees was, "If you would enter life, keep the commandments." The Ten Commandments couldn't save him, but love of money could *keep* him from eternal life. Only by obeying the command to put nothing (including money) above God could the man kick his money-obstacle out of the way.

NEEDLES ARE SMALL

Say this out loud: **wealth puts me at a big disadvantage.** If anyone heard you just now, I'm afraid they might be wondering what in the world you are reading. This is truly one of the most upside-down teachings of Jesus—especially for Comparison Girls of the western world. Yet if Jesus was willing to say to some first century Palestinians under Roman oppression, "Watch out! Be on your guard against all kinds of greed; life does not consist in an abundance of possessions" (Luke 12:15 NIV), I imagine he'd say the same thing to a group of modern women armed with credit cards.

So how can we overcome? How can we, with all our prosperity and excess, see money differently than the rich man who walked away? How can we stop shredding our napkins and storming off because we fear not getting what we want? How can we stop a camel-size disadvantage from keeping us from kingdom prosperity?

For a camel to go through a needle, it would have to become small. So small that it wouldn't be a camel anymore. In the world, money makes us big. In our wealth, we can look down with entitlement and order others around. But in the kingdom of heaven, we must become small. So small that we are transformed into something entirely different. "With man," Jesus tells us, "this is impossible, but with God all things are possible" (Matt. 19:26). Here's our reality. We *can't*, but God *can*.

Do you feel a little like the rich young man, gripping your rather full measuring cup with clammy hands, afraid that God might ask too much? Do you worry you won't be able to let go of something you have? If so, God kindly says, "You tip, I'll fill."

God doesn't tip our cup for us; he gives us the test and waits. But when we open wide our hands and pour out what he asks, he fills us with supernatural power. Yes, a camel is big and a needle is small. Yes, a woman with wealth is at a huge, camel-size disadvantage. But yes, God does the impossible every day of the week and empowers Comparison Girls to live by the spout. For example:

- When a woman opts out of a promotion at work so that she can spend more time serving at church, this is God doing the impossible.
- When a woman holds her spending accountable because she wants to steward God's money well, this is God doing the impossible.
- When a woman trusts in Jesus more than her homeowners insurance or bank account, this is God doing the impossible.
- When a woman makes God the owner and herself the servant—willing to give and share, this is God doing the impossible.
- And when a woman empties an earthly treasure into her heavenly account, this is God doing the impossible.

THE OTHER GRANDMA

Beth's adult daughter, her husband, and their kids live several hours away. When they come to town, they always stay with the *other* grandparents—the ones with lots of king-size beds and an in-ground pool. They also go on cruises and ski trips with the other grandparents, who always foot the bill.

Beth and her husband, Tom, live more simply than they did when their daughter was growing up. It's because God did the impossible and changed their minds about money. They moved into a smaller house and now live on a smaller budget—which allows for more generosity to the needy but fewer extravagant gifts and vacations with family.

Beth loves the giving projects she and Tom are involved in. She is content and filled with joy . . . except when she sees a photo of everyone gathered around the *other* grandma on a ski slope or white-sand beach. That's when the Comparison Girl anxiety creeps in.

Beth wonders, *Have we made the right choice? Perhaps we should spend money on big trips and a lavish home. Maybe then our kids would be drawn to us more.* But Beth has come to recognize her anxiety as a sure sign that she's back to focusing on the lines, measuring herself against the other grandma.

Beth and Tom want to love and serve God, not their money. The Lord hasn't given them peace about spending twenty thousand dollars on a week-long vacation, yet God *has* given them peace about giving generously. Beth knows her money is not just a blessing from God to enjoy but also a test of her faithfulness. Will she slip back into comparison? Will she measure the days her daughter's family spends with her versus the other grandma? Or will she continue to put God first and empty the extra in her pockets?

Comparison Girl, what is God asking you to do with the extra in your pockets? Rather than gripping your wealth with clammy hands, afraid that God might ask for too much, how will you tip your measuring cup? As you pour, invite God to fill you with the power to be generous.

≈ Can you relate to Beth's anxiety as she compared herself to the "other grandma"? Write down any situations causing you money stress right now. Beside each one, list ways your anxiety is tied to measuring up or fitting in. Write out any phrases from Luke 12:29–34 which offer you particular peace or focus.

≈ How is your surplus not just God's blessing but also his testing? What does Luke 16:11–12 say about the correlation between faithfulness on earth and "true riches" in heaven?

≈ Read Revelation 3:14–17. What similarities do you see between the church in Laodicea and your own community of believers?

≈ Read Luke 12:15–21. Rewrite the parable so that it ends with the rich man having treasure in heaven. Which version best represents you?

For Meditation: Luke 12:15 (NIV)

> Watch out! Be on your guard against all kinds of greed;
> life does not consist in an abundance of possessions.

Extra blessing is also an extra test from God. Will I open wide my hand and give away the extra God put in my pocket for someone else? *Lord, I want to trust you, not my bank account. I want to worship you, not this money. I want to serve you, not myself with what I have. Please do the impossible and help me give.*

Lesson 3: Rewards Slipping Through My Fingers
Read Matthew 19:16–30 and Luke 21:1–4

KIM IS A Southeast Asian woman who loves Jesus. When her husband sensed God leading them to start a seminary in an extremely poor district, Kim was reluctant. She had two young children, and this area isn't a place any of us would choose to move our families. But ultimately Kim said yes to God.

When they moved, Kim was first to get hired, so they agreed that she would work and her husband would develop the seminary and care for the children. Four years later, the seminary is a reality, and Kim still works the same job—with three quarters of her salary going toward the loan on the seminary's land. Kim's family lives on the other quarter in a one-room house, where they all share a single bed. There is no running water, and the closest well is over a kilometer away.

Life for Kim is hard, but my missionary friend Kristi—who met her at a women's retreat in Southeast Asia—says that when Kim led worship at the retreat, her face was aglow with joy. It was as if the room had cleared and Kim had transcended to the presence of Jesus. Kristi says it was some of the sweetest, purest worship that she's ever experienced.

Kim gives a different meaning to "working mom," don't you think? The Mommy War conversations—where moms face off and battle to prove that their way of mommy-ing is right—tempt me to compare myself in a way that's almost never helpful. But when I compare my life with Kim's, I'm inspired. She lives with her measuring cup tipped almost completely upside down, and yet she's full of supernatural joy!

THE JOY CONFLICT

Sometimes, especially when I want to buy something, I get the impression that pursuing joy is in direct conflict with following Jesus. I convince myself that to be happy, I must plug my ears to the Lord and just make the purchase. Swipe the credit card. If I asked Jesus, he would only tell me to deprive myself and be miserable. Except, as we've been learning, that isn't the case.

Jesus once told a little story about a man who sold everything he had (just as Jesus was telling the rich young man to do) so that he could buy a field with buried treasure. This man wasn't reluctant or sad the way the rich young man had been. He was full of *joy*. Now he could buy the field and have the treasure! (Matt. 13:44).

Like the man who gave up everything to buy what looked—to the casual observer—like an empty field, we also invest in a place hidden from the naked eye. Refusing to focus on the comparison lines, we pour everything out. We sacrifice knowing that our rewards are coming. But we don't sacrifice joy; we find it.

I love the detail that Mark adds when telling of Jesus's encounter with the rich young man: "And Jesus, looking at him, *loved him*, and said to him, 'You lack one thing: go, sell all that you have and give to the poor'" (Mark 10:21, emphasis added). Jesus looks at us with love, too, when he asks us to tip our measuring cups to the extreme. He doesn't want us to miss out; not now and not in the kingdom to come.

WHAT PETER ASKED

Peter waited (I hope) until the rich young man was out of earshot, then asked Jesus, "See, we have left everything and followed you. What then will we have?" (Matt. 19:27) Maybe *that* guy wasn't willing to leave everything behind, but these twelve already *had*.

Peter, Andrew, James, and John left their fishing business after the most lucrative catch ever (Luke 5:4–11). Matthew left the upscale life of tax collecting (Matt. 9:9). They had all left someone or something behind to follow Jesus. So when Jesus said to the rich young man, "Sell what you possess and give to the poor, and you will have treasure in heaven" (Matt. 19:21), Peter wondered if the promise applied to them too.

I'm glad Peter asked, because I also want to know, but I'm almost afraid Jesus will chide him. Isn't it a little greedy to be asking about rewards? Doesn't Jesus want us to pour out everything and expect nothing? Shouldn't we just get back to serving?

But no, Jesus doesn't chide Peter. Not for comparing himself with a foolish man, and not for asking about rewards. In fact, Jesus encourages Peter's question by describing the kingdom to come in vivid detail.

Jesus will sit on a glorious throne, and his disciples will be there too. Twelve thrones; one for each of them. They will have leadership responsibilities and positions of honor. And they will receive back not just one of everything they've given up, but a hundredfold. They will live this way, never experiencing loss again, for eternity.

Peter and the others were grinning widely at this point. I'm sure of it. And maybe they were getting choked up a bit, too, because not only had Jesus noticed what they had given up and left behind; he was keeping detailed accounts. There was math involved.

If everything gets multiplied by one hundred, a hundred dollars becomes $10,000. A thousand dollars becomes $100,000. And that's when the disciples realize. The guy walking away isn't the wealthy one. *They are.* They are filthy rich!

Does Jesus chide us for being strategic about storing up wealth? No, he's saying that's *exactly* what we should do—just not on earth.

Considering the Angle

In his book *The Treasure Principal*, Randy Alcorn compares our money here on earth to eternal investment capital. He says, "Every day is an opportunity to buy up more shares in His kingdom. *You can't take it with you, but you can send it on ahead.*"[6]

That's very motivating, but what if your measuring cup doesn't have much to pour out? You might say, "My cup is so empty, I'd have to tip it almost all the way to pour out even a few drops!" Friend, Jesus sees you and cares when you feel you have so little to give. Listen to this.

Once when a poor widow put only two copper coins into the offering box, he called his disciples over and pointed her out, saying, "Truly, I tell you, this poor widow has put in more than all of them. For they all contributed out of their abundance, but she out of her poverty put in all she had to live on" (Luke 21:3–4).

Did you catch that she "put in more"? *More* is a comparison word. Jesus is saying that if a billionaire puts a million dollars in the offering plate and you sacrificially put your last dollar in beside the million, you have given more. Jesus could call his disciples over to be inspired by *you*. **With heaven's eternal rewards, there's math involved, but one plus one doesn't always equal two.** Sacrifice gives your small gift more weight.

Another time Jesus said, "Whoever gives one of these little ones even a cup of cold water because he is a disciple, truly, I say to you, he will by no means lose his reward" (Matt. 10:42). I always picture someone giving a toddler a miniature paper cup of water when I read that verse. Jesus wants us to know that no copper coin goes unnoticed, and no two-cent cup of water is unaccounted for. Each time we defy selfishness and tip our measuring cups forward to pour out even a few drops, we send treasure on ahead to the place "where moths and rust cannot destroy, and thieves do not break in and steal" (Matt. 6:20 NLT).

You know, Satan is a regular visitor to this heavenly place where moth and rust can't destroy things.[7] Jesus *lives* there and knows exactly what awaits us, but Satan has a good idea. So while our Lord looks at us with love, wanting us to pursue treasure in his kingdom (Mark 10:21), Satan—the deceiver—wants to distract us with our own selfishness. So he prowls about on the earth, whispering, "Look at her house. And how does she afford that outfit, much less that car?" Then he grins wickedly as we go scampering off in our jealousy, greed, and measure-up frenzy.

Living by faith is what God rewards. Living by sight—fixated on the here and now—is how we let the rewards slip through our fingers. Randy Alcorn admits that this isn't popular to talk about, but Christians can lose out on heavenly rewards. He says, "Scripture is clear. Not all Christians will hear the master say, 'Well done, good and faithful servant' (Matt. 25:23). Not all of us will have treasure in heaven (Matt. 6:19–21). Not all of us will have the same position of authority in heaven (Luke 19:17, 19, 26). We will have differing levels of reward in heaven

(1 Cor. 3:12–15). There is no sign that, once given or withheld, rewards are anything other than eternal and irrevocable."[8]

That last sentence is important, so don't miss it, dear sister. There are eternal consequences for what you choose to do with your measuring cup. If you've been plugging your ears to Jesus's voice so you can swipe your credit card and "be happy," perhaps it's time to consider what Jesus says awaits on the other side.

MORE THAN FAIR

Jesus used a red-letter comparison to seal this conversation about rewards. He told his disciples, "But many who are first will be last, and the last first" (Matt. 19:30).

Red-Letter Comparison: "But many who are first will be last, and the last first" (Matt. 19:30).

The rich young man would've come in "first" on many a comparison list. No doubt, people looked at his sprawling wealth and whined, "It's not fair." And for the disciples who are about to became hated, crucified, and exiled because of Jesus, life *certainly* wasn't fair. But Jesus wants us all to know that there is coming a day when things will be more than fair. We'll all receive far more than we deserve.

God, who sees everything and misses nothing, will reward every sacrifice, down to the two-cent paper cup of water. Of course, we won't be rewarded for the times we wasted things or made costly, foolish choices. But to the extent that we've suffered loss for Jesus's sake, we will be glad we did.

Perhaps you read this and are thrilled with what's ahead. Or maybe, like me, you're thinking, "Uh . . . hold up. I'm not sure I've poured out nearly enough yet." Either way, as we think about the future, Jesus urges us to tip our cups forward and be strategic. Like the guy who sold everything to buy a treasure hidden from view, Jesus encourages us to invest in heaven and dream big.

DREAM BIG

After Bible study, the twelve of us are still at the table chatting while the teacher is packing up. And that's when a tall, beautiful woman comes running—not walking—into the room. We can tell instantly that she's not your typical visitor who got the time wrong. Her security guards, who ran right in with her, are our first clue. And our second is the way her manicured style from head to toe is exactly on point.

"Teacher!" she cries, then collapses at his feet, not caring what we think. "I was so afraid I would miss you. You have to help me. I've been having these nightmares. I'm afraid to die. I'm terrified, really. I think about it all the time. And someone told me that you tell people how to live forever. Can you tell me what to do?"

Jesus says kindly, "You've heard of the Ten Commandments?" She says, "Yes, I keep those always. But what else? How can I get this life after death?" Jesus looks at her with love in his eyes and says, "Go and liquidate everything. Sell your business. Sell each of your homes. Shut down your Instagram and delete your followers. Give it all away to charity and live a private, quiet life. Then come back and join this Bible study."

The woman looks horrified. Tears escape. Extreme sadness washes over her face. She stands up and somberly walks out of the room with her security guards close behind.

We're stunned. Then one of us leans in and says with great intensity, "Jesus, I have a question. We've *done* that. We've given up everything to be your followers. Riley's whole family won't have any contact with her. Karla gave up a career because you told her to raise a family. Jan's getting ready to go overseas to do church planting. All of us have given up something. That woman wasn't willing, but we *are*. Will there be any rewards for us?"

Our Lord smiles and says, "That's exactly the right question. And the answer is *yes*."

Dream big, dear sisters. With eyes of faith, dream big about where God is asking you to sacrifice. Dream about who might need what's in your measuring cup. Just think of the rewards that await those who tip their measuring cups forward and let generosity flow.

≈ Tell about a time that you looked at someone's wealth and thought, "It's not fair." How does the "more than fair" return on investment of Matthew 19:29 encourage you?

≈ Read 1 Timothy 6:17–19 and list out the instructions given. What reward is promised?

≈ Make a list of the ways you have suffered loss for Jesus's sake. Beside your list, in bold letters, write, "He loves me. He's keeping track. He will reward me."

≈ Read 2 Corinthians 9:6–8. Have you been sowing generously or sparingly? How is Jesus inviting you to respond? What attitude does he want you to have (v. 7)?

For Meditation: Matthew 19:30

But many who are first will be last, and the last first.

Jesus doesn't chide me for asking about rewards in heaven. He encourages me to think strategically and let my generosity flow. *Lord, I will stop plugging my ears and joyfully dream big about the sacrifices you'd like me to make.*

Chapter Four
Comparing Skin-Deep Packaging

THERE'S A GROUP of women known in their community as the "Real Housewives of Smallville." These women live in an ordinary, smallish town, so they don't have TV cameras trailing behind them, capturing their lives for a reality show. But here's their reality: They each have classy wardrobes, manicured nails, and beautiful, fit bodies. They are often spotted sliding out of their black Denalis to drop kids off at football or to run in the grocery store with their hair done, makeup on, and bootie-hugging leggings—as if they are perpetually on their way to a filmed yoga class. And maybe they are. But yoga isn't the only thing helping these young moms maintain their bikini bodies.

Rumor has it that each one has undergone shape-enhancing surgery over the past couple of years. They're all set for their spring break photo, all lined up together on the edge of the pool. No doubt they'll each add #blessed to their Instagram posts.

When I think about this group of women, my first thought is, "I'd like to interview one of them." Behind closed doors and hidden away from the others, I'd like to hear one group member tell me about the pressure she feels to keep her weight down, highlights up, wrinkles away, and wardrobe in sync with the others. I'd like to know about the exhaustion she feels when she falls into bed and the stress when she rises to live another day pushing herself to keep up. I'd also like to know what makes a group of beautiful friends all individually decide to schedule plastic surgery.

I'm sure that the pressure these women feel, both inside and outside their social circle, is very valid and very real. But Jesus relieved the pressure of our measure-up-in-the-mirror agendas. He said that we don't have to look great to be great.

Comparing our skin-deep packaging brings all sorts of stress and angst. As we obsess in front of the mirror, it's the eyes of other people we're worried about. How do we look? How will they see us? What if they *do* see us? What if they *don't*? In this chapter, we'll learn to look at ourselves in the mirror through Jesus's upside-down eyes. Instead of being consumed with our reflections, we'll learn to turn from the mirror with new confidence, ready to place me-free focus on the ones we're called to serve.

Lesson 1: A Security Deeper Than Skin
Read Matthew 4:23–5:11, 6:25–34, and 7:24–27

WHEN RACHEL WAS in high school, her parents taught her that she was special: a treasure created by God. She was worth waiting for. And she believed them. Rachel cherished the idea that maybe someone special truly was waiting for her too. She would keep waiting on God, trusting him, and believing the truth about herself. That was her plan.

Then one Friday night after a football game, Rachel came to the stinging conclusion that her plan was flawed. Her dad pulled into the school parking lot, and after she slid into his car, she watched out the back window as several of her closest friends—all beautiful, popular cheerleaders—were meeting up with their "special someones" before going to the dance. Yet there was no special someone watching for her.

Rachel came to believe that she was a minus in a world of pluses, and all of her waiting, trusting, and believing was never going to turn her into a plus. Her faith in Jesus was never going to offer a measuring-cup advantage, so she needed a new game plan. A new strategy. Bottom line, Rachel *had* to get to the dance. Which meant she *had* to get into a dress size that matched the ones her friends were wearing. Rachel made a choice, there in the back of her dad's car, to take a break from working on inside beauty. She was going to get to work on the part of her everybody else could see.

Do you ever feel like a minus in a world of pluses? Do you worry that your appearance is holding you back? Are you driven to change how you look so you can get what you want and measure up? Rachel didn't realize it then, but her enemy had just used comparison to entice her into fifteen years of bondage and food addiction. I'll tell you more of her story in lesson 3, but for now I'd like you to consider whether your enemy is using your appearance-comparing habit as a trap.

Our culture puts so much emphasis on how we look. We're confronted with images of flawless faces, flat tummies, and slightly curved hips everywhere we turn. For Comparison Girls, there is such pain in falling short. There is such enticement to focus on the lines. And there is such bondage in our obsession to finally measure up—or in this case, our obsession to slim down.

#BLESSED

I love the fact that Jesus preaches his "Ribbon Cutting Sermon"[1] not to a crowd of beautiful, high profile people, the way you might expect for the launch of a great movement. Instead, Jesus made his grand announcement of the good news of the kingdom standing before the sick, hurting, poor, and marginalized—those who felt like minuses in a world of pluses. Here's how Matthew describes the crowd gathering for this sermon:

> And they brought him all the sick, those afflicted with various diseases and pains, those oppressed by demons, those having seizures, and paralytics, and he healed them. And great crowds followed him. . . . Seeing the crowds, he went up on the mountain . . . and he opened his mouth and taught them, saying, "Blessed are the poor in spirit, for theirs is the kingdom of heaven. Blessed are those who mourn, for they shall be comforted . . ." (Matt. 4:24–5:4)

The people in this crowd were not the ones you'd look out a back window and become jealous of. You'd never look into their measuring cups and consider them blessed. As Jesus snips the ribbon and swings open the gate, he points out just how sharp the contrast is between his kingdom and our measure-up world by opening his sermon with a string of "Blessed are . . ." statements. I challenge you to find one thing listed in Matthew 5:3–11 that you would feel comfortable snapping a photo of, then adding #blessed to.

Yet as Jesus looked out on these epileptics, paralytics, and people with chronic pain, he saw that they *were* blessed, because their suffering had brought them to *him*. Friend, is there some physical suffering that has led you to Jesus? What about emotional suffering or stress over how you look? Whether it's over an extra ten pounds or an extra eighty, whether because of scars or thinning hair, whether due to severe acne or extreme wrinkles, **Jesus wants you to bring your agony and distress about your skin-deep packaging to him.** Whatever brings you to tears can also bring you closer to him—and that's the only way for your heartache to be healed.

APPEARANCE ANXIETY

These people who had gathered were the outcasts and less-thans, so they were understandably hurting and anxious. Jesus comforted them by explaining that in the kingdom, things are different. Measure-up fear and get-ahead pride both get checked at the door. The way to be great isn't by fitting into size two jeans or catching a man's eye. Here you become great when you *stop* living by the lines.

If you're a Comparison Girl who is in pain or even crisis because of how your skin-deep packaging compares to everybody else, please note that obviously the people in Jesus's crowd were stressed about similar issues. "Why are you anxious about clothing?" (Matt. 6:28), Jesus asked. Then he called attention to the grass, waving in the wind, which was adorned with colorful, ruffled lilies. The grass hadn't been working, fretting, or sewing to come up with eye-pleasing attire; God dressed the grass. *If God makes the grass beautiful, won't he do the same for us?* Jesus asked.

This anxiety-quelling logic can be mine today, right now, yet here's my sobering reality. After listening to Jesus explain that God is trustworthy and loves to make me beautiful, I can decide to worry and fret about my appearance anyway. I don't usually think of it as a decision; it feels like I don't have a choice. But here's the question. Is Jesus my king? Do his words matter to me? **Am I going to build my life on Jesus's upside-down promises?**

A HIDDEN FOUNDATION

As I stood chatting at a friend's house one day, I asked, "Does it look like that person's chimney is tilting?"

I wasn't imagining things. In the weeks to come, a thin line of daylight appeared between the house and its beautiful stone chimney, which used to be attached. Over time, the tilt became more pronounced until one morning—with creaking, groaning, and cracking noises, it collapsed. The beautiful stone chimney now lay in a giant heap of rocks. I learned later that the builder had cut corners and not laid a foundation. He built a two-ton chimney on shifting sand . . . literally.

Jesus closed his Ribbon Cutting Sermon with a comparison story about a wise man who built his house with a foundation and a foolish man who built his with none. When the storm came, the wise man's house stood strong, but the foolish man's house fell with a great, creaking collapse. The difference between the two? The wise man listened and did what Jesus said. He let Jesus's words matter, and he built his life on Jesus's promises. The foolish man did not.

We see the same contrast among Comparison Girls who are focused on skin-deep packaging. The foolish woman refuses to listen to Jesus's anxiety-quelling logic about the grass and the lilies. She insists on turning to her mirror to build her beauty—using makeup, fashion, gym memberships, and diets. Yet without a moment's notice, the winds of cancer or aging or weight gain can come blowing through the foolish woman's life and bring great collapse to her beauty. She knows this. So her anxiety in front of the mirror is based on very real risk. She had no control over storms and no way to ultimately keep her beauty from failing. So she just keeps building and worrying. Building and worrying.

But there is a wise woman whose beauty is less about how she looks and more about who she trusts. She's the one who *does* listen to Jesus when he talks about the grass and the lilies and does believe that her Father cares (Matt. 6:30). She entrusts her wardrobe—regardless of what size or how trendy her clothing is—to the one who knit together the body she's trying to outfit. Her trust in God spreads like a foundation beneath her closet, her mirror, and her whole life (Ps. 18:2). It's not that she neglects her appearance. Perhaps she does diet or wear makeup or shop for flattering clothes. But a wise woman's most important beauty work is not in front of a mirror; it's before the Lord. As she puts her trust in what God says about her, she builds a foundation which will hold her firm regardless of what storms come. So she keeps building and trusting. Building and trusting.

Remember how fifteen-year-old Rachel decided to get to work on the part of her everybody could see? Friends, Rachel would tell you that this is when she lost her footing. God wants us to cultivate the type of beauty that's hidden. It's the foundation, resting below the part everybody sees. First Peter 3:4 says, "Let your adorning be the hidden person of the heart with the imperishable beauty of a gentle and quiet spirit, which in God's sight is very precious." The woman who has this imperishable beauty may or may not be beautiful on the outside. But to her, the lines are irrelevant. She's not anxious or worried about how she measures up. Her hidden foundation of trust in God makes her *free*.

WHEN VALLEYS BECOME HILLS

In her book, *The Scars That Have Shaped Me*, Vaneetha Risner tells about longing for a perfect body as a teen. She wanted to be accepted, but what she found in the mirror wasn't acceptable. Her twenty-one operations could not undo what polio had done. She felt defective and inadequate, and she had the scars to prove it.

Then in her thirties, Vaneetha's body failed her again. She developed post-polio syndrome, which caused pain and escalating weakness. It also caused her husband of seventeen years to leave their family. "God, why do you hate me?" Vaneetha would sometimes scream into the darkness. The pain of lost independence, rejection, and fear ripped through her like a hurricane, threatening her very foundation.

Vaneetha's life has been shaped by physical and emotional scars, but her encounters with God during her lowest moments in life have been even more shaping. A mentor once suggested that Vaneetha chart her life's highs and lows, and when she did, she was surprised by the pattern that emerged. The times she was at her lowest were the times she was closest to God. It was almost as if, from God's perspective, the timeline could be flipped upside down, so that the valleys were actually hills—lifting her up, closer to him.[2]

Have you ever charted your hills and valleys? Have you noticed that your lowest points have brought you closest to God? Jesus's Ribbon Cutting Sermon was preached to people who had been living in the measure-up valley. Yet the things that brought them to tears also brought them to him—and because of that, he said they were blessed.

Jesus repeatedly said the first will be last and the last will be first in his kingdom. Consider that red-letter comparison in regard to skin-deep packaging. Which women come to mind first when I ask, "Who has been blessed with beauty?" You might think of cover models or movie stars. Or perhaps you think of the most beautiful women in your family, workplace, or church. But what if there's a correlation between those who come to mind *first* and those who are *last* to humble themselves and seek Jesus?

When our measuring cup has more—especially more beauty—we Comparison Girls tend to put our security in whatever sets us apart or lifts us up. Yet finding self-worth in reflective glass or finding security in the eyes of an admirer is like building a house on shifting sand. A storm could come without a moment's notice and wash away every trace of our beauty. But Jesus wants us to have rock-solid security, which can never be washed away by a storm.

Jesus loves us and wants to provide every bit of assurance we need. So when our scars, stretchmarks, extra weight, and wrinkles draw us to his presence, they are blessings in the truest sense. Friends, you and I need a load-bearing foundation. We need solid-rock truth to hold us firm. We need *Jesus*. Let's be wise women who listen to truth, who build a foundation of trust on Jesus, and who cultivate hidden beauty that lasts.

≈ That night in her dad's car, Rachel decided to take a break from working on inner beauty and turned her focus to the beauty everybody could see. What would you say to Rachel that night if you had the chance? Which of your own appearance goals do you need to rethink? How is God convicting you to stop living by "the lines"?

≈ List any "storms" that have threatened your security in front of the mirror. Weight gain? Chemotherapy? A husband's affair? Singleness? What truths have formed a foundation for you? Write Psalm 18:2 as a prayer to God, your rock.

≈ Read 2 Corinthians 4:16–18. How have you experienced outer "wasting away"? How does fixing your eyes on the unseen kingdom of God help you to become renewed day by day?

≈ Read 1 Peter 3:3–4. What are you doing to cultivate inner beauty? Write out this verse and place it near your mirror to remind you to build a beneath-the-surface foundation.

For Meditation: 2 Corinthians 4:16 (NIV)

> Therefore we do not lose heart. Though outwardly we are wasting away, yet inwardly we are being renewed day by day.

My most important beauty work is done not in front of the mirror but in the part of me that nobody can see. My trust in God spreads like a foundation beneath my closet, my mirror, and my life. *Jesus, I want to leave my measure-up mindset behind and build my life on what you say matters— which is less about how I look and more about whom I trust.*

Lesson 2: To Be Seen
Read Matthew 23:1–12

ONCE WHEN OUR family was climbing Sleeping Bear Dunes here in Michigan, I looked at a woman up ahead and thought, *I wonder if that's the way I look from behind.* The woman was about my size, so I decided to ask for my five-year-old daughter's opinion.

Softly, I said, "Linds, is that lady skinnier or fatter than Mommy?" Always happy to help, Lindsay stopped climbing and began looking back and forth between the other woman and me, trying to size us up. "Uhhhh . . ." she said after a few rounds of evaluations, "I think you're just a yiddle fatter, Mommy. But just a yiddle bit!"

What a ridiculous game I was playing (and still do). In the middle of a gorgeous display of creation, rather than enjoying my great big God under wide skies and sloping sand dunes, I was a Comparison Girl asking a five-year-old to measure me against a stranger.

JESUS CALLS FOR AN INTERVENTION

Jesus wasn't oblivious to the way we worry about how we look to others, from the front or behind. In fact, in his Ribbon Cutting Sermon (which we looked at in the previous lesson), Jesus issued several warnings against trying to impress people (Matt. 6:1–18). As he preached, Jesus didn't call out the habits of the religious leaders, but the showy examples he chose—like blowing a trumpet before giving to the needy or praying loudly on the street corner—pointed a finger straight at them.

In today's lesson we're going to skip forward to a time when Jesus's interactions with the religious leaders have progressed way past implicit rebuke. It's now the Tuesday morning before Jesus will be executed, and he is speaking to a crowd of his disciples gathered at the temple for the Passover celebration (see Matt. 23:1; 24:1). Though Jesus is fully aware that the religious leaders are plotting to kill him, he isn't hiding or defending himself. Instead, he cares enough to call for an intervention.

An intervention is when we confront someone we love who is making grievous choices and warn them to turn back. We see the consequences up ahead, and we're willing to stand in the middle of the road and say, "Stop! No, don't!" That's what Jesus is doing as he calls out seven forceful warnings or "woes" to the scribes and Pharisees, there in the temple courts (Matt. 23:1–36).[3]

I'm sure that it was awkward. I'm sure the disciples in the crowd were glancing around, wondering if the leaders were in earshot. And what provoked Jesus's loud rebukes? It was the nasty habit the scribes and Pharisees had of trying to impress people and draw attention to themselves. Jesus said, "They do all their deeds to be seen by others" (Matt. 23:5).

This rebuke is a bit awkward for us, too, because there are also women among us who are desperate to be seen. We can tell by their extreme efforts to attract everyone's attention with their style, whether that's by always looking flawlessly put together or always wearing dark clothing and a surly expression. *But is an intervention really necessary, Jesus?* we ask. We certainly don't want anyone to call an intervention with that anxious woman staring back from the bathroom mirror.

As we listen to some of the harshest warnings from Jesus's Tuesday morning address, let me encourage you not to make the mistake of saying, "Oh, this problem isn't *that* bad." Obviously, Jesus thought it was. Nor should we assume that the warnings don't apply to us, since that's obviously what the scribes and Pharisees thought. As Jesus exposed the underbelly of their longing to be admired, they closed their ears, stiffened their backs, and firmed their resolve to murder him.

RECEIVING THREE WARNINGS

We don't always try to impress people the same way the religious leaders did, of course, but consider this. We're being deceived by the same enemy who deceived them. We're being tempted with the same measure-up desire to look good in the eyes of others, while disregarding the eyes of God. As those who love Jesus and want to follow him, let's learn from the mistakes these religious leaders made and do exactly what they wouldn't. Let's receive these warnings of Jesus and allow him to shine a spotlight on our ugly desire to be seen.

Here are three specifics that Jesus warned against:

Dressing to Call Attention

"They do all their deeds to be seen by others. For they make their phylacteries broad and fringes long," Jesus said (Matt. 23:5). Phylacteries are little leather-covered boxes which Jewish men—still today—tie onto their foreheads and arms. The boxes have little mini scrolls inside with portions of God's Word. This is their way of *literally* practicing God's instructions to "fix these words of mine in your hearts and minds; tie them as symbols on your hands and bind them on your foreheads" (Deut. 11:18 NIV; see also Exod. 13:9, 16; Deut. 6:8).

Reread that verse and notice the irony. God wanted them to fix his words on the *inside*—in their hearts and minds. But they put the words on the *outside* where everyone could see. They wanted their phylacteries wider than the next guy's to draw attention to themselves.

Same with the "fringes," which were tassels that they put on the corners of their garments to remind them of God's commands. Yet rather than having their attention drawn to God, the religious leaders had extra-long tassels, which drew attention to *themselves*.

Are there ways that we also dress to call attention to ourselves? We don't wear tight, low-cut, see-through clothing because it's comfortable. And we don't pay triple for a name brand because the little logo is pretty. And even when we wear buttoned-up, flowy, floor-length dresses, aren't we sometimes trying to draw attention to our superior modesty? When we use our clothes to draw the eyes of others, we're no different than the guys strapping leather boxes to their heads.

Positioning Ourselves to Be Seen

Whether at banquets or in the worship services, the scribes and Pharisees wanted to position themselves to be in everyone's line of sight. They wanted to be spotted, to stand out, to be admired.

Are there ways we position ourselves to be seen too? The photos we post. The place we sit in church. The group shots we want to be included in. When we posture ourselves to be noticed, it's obvious that we're living by the lines.

Loving Public Admiration

The Pharisees did not hope to blend in around town or at the market. No, they lived for that moment when someone would call out using big titles so they could receive big recognition. They loved being called "rabbi" so that everyone in earshot would know they were a big shot.

And what about us? With the dawn of social media, our love for public admiration has only grown more public. We live for comments like, "Dang, girl!" Or "You look like their sister, not their mom!" Our acquired "likes" are approval tally marks. And the lack thereof is proof the other way.

THE PACKAGING ISN'T THE PROBLEM

Perhaps you (like me) had never heard of phylacteries, let alone broad ones. Obviously, the phylacteries and tassels weren't the problem. What they were wearing and where they were sitting simply exposed the real problem, which was in their hearts. These religious leaders craved admiration. More than anything in life, they wanted to be seen. They drove themselves to ridiculous lengths—including lengthy tassels and big boxes on their heads—and they were withering under all of their self-imposed requirements. Yet in all of their ambition to find approval in each other's eyes, they completely lacked any regard for *God's* eyes.

It's the same with us. The clothes we're wearing, the selfies we're taking, and the tears we're shedding on our bathroom scale only expose the *real* problem, which is in our hearts. Like the Pharisees, we long to be admired, and since we know that our culture puts a premium on thin bodies and pretty faces, that's what we measure. Our eyes run like laser tape measures, instantly taking measurements of every person we encounter and every image we're exposed to. And the billions of dollars we spend each year on cosmetics, weight loss, and cosmetic surgery reveal how invested we are in our own "packaging."

For some of us, our obsession is maintaining the beauty we've cultivated. We'd rather die than watch our beauty fade. For others of us, our obsession is concealing defects and deficiencies. We're extremely insecure about being seen and would rather die than be photographed unawares. Either way, our me-focused drive is what withers away at our inner beauty, which can only be cultivated by a quiet hope and trust in God.

Mirror-Free

Recently my daughter, Lindsay, who is now a college student, gave up wearing makeup for Lent. But then she realized that all her trips to the mirror throughout the day to obsess over her makeup-less appearance were defeating the purpose. Lent is a time to give something up and refocus on God, but Lindsay was constantly refocusing on herself. Her exercise in less self-focus wasn't working. So she readjusted her commitment and gave up "mirror time" instead of makeup. She looked into the mirror while applying makeup, but that was it. No checking her outfit from all angles. No checking her hair between classes. No looking up while she washed her hands in the bathroom.

Lindsay was surprised at the amount of time she was accustomed to spending evaluating herself in front of her mirror. And she hadn't realized how her comparisons throughout the day were measured against her reflection that morning. Without "mirror time" she found new freedom. She could say, "Wow, my friend Lacy looks so pretty today," and not compare Lacy's outfit, hair, or makeup with her own.

There's a certain correlation between how obsessed we are with our own appearance and how free we are to focus on other people. The more me-focused we are in the mirror, the more me-focused we'll be when we turn toward others. The greater our obsession with the lines (which in this case include the lines of our bodies), the less free we are to focus on the spout.

The Antidote

As a culture, our anxiety issues seem to be keeping pace with the spread of digital media. The more we see airbrushed perfection, the more we want it for ourselves. Since we are consumed more than ever with how we look compared with how other people look, Jesus's forceful "intervention" language seems quite apropos. If you, like me, recognize that you're far too wrapped up in appearances, I invite you to slip once more into Jesus's Tuesday morning audience. He's just about to share the anxiety-relieving antidote to this enslaving desire we often have to be seen and admired. Ready for another red-letter comparison?

Jesus said, "The greatest among you shall be your servant. Whoever exalts himself will be humbled, and whoever humbles himself will be exalted" (Matt. 23:11–12). Don't miss this, friends. In response to some people who are obsessed with their measure-up appearances, Jesus offers this as the antidote: self-forgetful serving.

Red-Letter Comparison: Whoever exalts herself will be humbled, and whoever humbles herself will be exalted (see Matt. 23:12).

In your mind's eye, gather all the Christian women you know into Jesus's crowd. Add the woman who is intimidatingly beautiful. Add the one who needs a little fashion advice. Add me in, too, as one who's fairly average. Now look around and listen as Jesus tells all of us that our greatness isn't based on what we look like. This means that the most athletic and bronzed among us aren't necessarily the greatest. Nor are the ones with the prettiest faces, firmest thighs, or classiest wardrobes. And in fact, those of us who are trying to exalt ourselves with our stand-out attractiveness are not actually achieving greatness—not in Jesus's kingdom. Instead, the great ones among us are those who serve. The exalted ones in our group are the ones who humble themselves and focus on others instead of obsessing about themselves. Knowing this, dear friends, is the antidote to comparison's poison. It's the way to healing and freedom.

Some of us have been exhausting ourselves with regimented eating plans. Others of us have been exhausting our resources to acquire the right clothes and makeup. Many of us have abused our bodies with excessive exercise or eating disorders. We have cried and hated and self-loathed and withdrawn—all because of our obsession to measure up.

But Jesus wants us to enjoy our bodies and love our unique physical design. We're *supposed* to be different shapes, sizes, and colors. He calls us to unity, not uniformity, remember? Bondage and distance form when we compare up in insecurity or compare down in superiority. Unity and connection form when we humbly lay aside our measure-up perfectionism.

Friend, if you're ready to be free of the withering effects of me-focus, then glance around the crowd once more, but rather than comparing how you look with others, ask, "How can I serve someone here?" Servants aren't trying to be seen. They aren't afraid of being seen either. They're too busy looking for ways to invest in others to worry about how and whether others are looking at them.

Serving doesn't change what we look like, but it does change how we look at each other and ourselves.

Summer's Explant

Summer recently had surgery to remove her breast implants. She did so partly because of the way the implants were negatively affecting her health but also because of what is happening in her heart.

It was five years ago, after a time of post-partum depression and spiritual drift, that Summer elected to have implant surgery. Though she loved her new baby, Summer loathed the effects of childbearing on her body. And though she never would have admitted it, the breast augmentation was Summer's solution to a lifetime of comparing and trying to measure up. Summer didn't like the way she looked, and this was something she could do about it.

Summer now sees that the implant surgery was saying something about her heart—yet so does the explant surgery. Over the past five years, Summer sees how God has reshaped her inner self, as she has responded to him by shifting her focus to others and away from herself. She left a career she loved to invest full-time in her marriage and parenting. And she spends her me-time leading Bible studies and sharing what God has taught her about humility, serving, and love.

As Summer invests in other people, her drive to please the Lord is melting her drive to be eye-pleasing. She's finding freedom from her appearance bondage. When Summer had the explant surgery, it was like leaving the chains of her measure-up, body-image bondage on the operating table. She felt a *freedom* to return to her natural, God-given shape.

Friend, is Jesus calling for an intervention? Is he asking you to lay down your consuming desire to be seen as perfectly beautiful? Or to relax your expectations for how you look? If you are burdened with me-focused concern over your appearance, here's the antidote: become like Jesus, who focused on others, not himself, saying, "I am among you as the one who serves" (Luke 22:27).

≈ Have you experienced any bondage (eating disorders, exercise obsession, anxiety, etc.) from comparison? Have you ever distanced yourself from someone because of what they look like compared with you?

≈ Read Genesis 11:1–9. How does this story parallel with Matthew 23:5 and 12?

≈ Do you see a correlation between how obsessed you are with your appearance and how free you are to focus on others? Read Philippians 2:3–4. How could self-forgetful serving provide an antidote for measure-up worry or pride related to how you look?

≈ Read Matthew 6:1–6, 16–18 and list the ways that the Pharisees tried to "be seen." What do these verses say about rewards for things that are seen by others versus things that are unseen? What is God showing you about striving for physical beauty?

≈ Scroll through your Instagram or Facebook app (or you can file through your memory) until you come across a woman you would ordinarily be tempted to measure yourself against. Say aloud, "The great ones are the servants." Instead of comparing your size, shape, skin, or hair with this woman's, ask, "How can I serve her today?" Ask God to show you a way to serve, encourage, or lift her up—either online or in person.

For Meditation: Luke 22:27

I am among you as the one who serves.

As a servant, I'm not trying to be seen, nor am I afraid of being seen. I'm too busy investing in others to worry about how I measure up in their eyes. *Lord, rather than seeking to be noticed or admired by others, I want to become one of the great ones who serves.*

Lesson 3: The Inside of the Cup
Read Matthew 23:1–12, 25–26 and Luke 11:37–41

AFTER RACHEL (WHOM we met in lesson 1) watched her friends heading to the dance without her, she decided to make some drastic efforts to "fix" herself.

Radical dieting. Extreme exercise. Starvation-prompted binging. Then purging to undo the damage. The pattern became addictive. Because of her obsessions, Rachel began to withdraw and be excluded, which was the opposite of what she hoped for. She quickly became depressed, isolated, and stuck. Thankfully she let someone know she needed help.

While counseling was helpful, for Rachel it wasn't healing. After trying several treatment plans, she came to the quiet conclusion: *I think I'm not fixable. I'm going to just try to live with it and not talk about it.* So that's what she did. For years.

On the outside Rachel looked good to others, but inside she was filled with turmoil and disappointment. As a girl she had planned to follow Jesus in victory, but as an adult she was living in defeat. In measure-up desperation, Rachel was still consumed with cleaning herself up on the outside. But she didn't involve God, and without him it's impossible to clean up on the inside.

DISHWASHING PRACTICES

Twice Jesus used the analogy of washing the outside of a cup or dish but ignoring the inside. One instance was at the temple that Tuesday before his crucifixion. Jesus gave his seven woes to the religious leaders, including this one: "Woe to you, scribes and Pharisees, hypocrites! For you clean the outside of the cup and the plate, but inside they are full of greed and self-indulgence" (Matt. 23:25).

The other instance came earlier in Jesus's ministry, when he was invited to a Pharisee's home for dinner. When he arrived, Jesus went straight to the table without washing first, which caused the Pharisee and his friends to react with disgust-factor astonishment.

The Pharisees didn't just think cleanliness was next to godliness; they thought it *was* godliness. Remember, they were the experts on God's law, which was full of clean and unclean rules. Touching certain things could make you unclean so you'd have to purify yourself according to the law's specifics (see Lev. 15). The Pharisees, however, added their own ceremonial rules including the wash-your-hands-before-you-eat one (Matt. 15:2). They made it seem like their meticulous clean-up efforts were aimed at pleasing God, but really they just wanted to seem pious.

This is what was going on when "the Pharisee was astonished to see that [Jesus] did not first wash before dinner" (Luke 11:38). Notice that as he reclined at the table, here's what Jesus didn't do. He didn't play along and get up to wash his hands. Nor did he overlook the disgust in the Pharisees' eyes, all peacemaker-like. Jesus is not supportive when people press others to meet some standard that God never set, or react in self-appointed disgust.

Comparison Girl, stop a moment and consider. Are you guilty of this? Do your friends or loved ones feel pressured to clean up according to your standards, not God's? To wear stylish clothes, shed extra pounds, or keep their hair and beards trimmed tidy? Or do they dress modestly to please *you*, not the Lord? If so, please seat yourself at the table, because Jesus has something to say:

> You Pharisees cleanse the outside of the cup and of the dish, but inside you are full of greed and wickedness. You fools! (Luke 11:39–40)

These Pharisees are incredibly foolish. Here they are, reclining at a table with Jesus, thinking *they're* the ones who are clean, when ironically it's their inner grime of pride and superiority driving them to have sudsy-clean hands. They want to measure up, not please God. And while they might look good to each other—seated at the table with their damp hands glimmering in the candlelight—Jesus saw their inner cups, caked with grimy filth.

My Cup's Inner Grime

There are obvious differences between the Pharisees' ambitions and my own, but at the core our problem is the same. Like them, my inner grime of desperately trying to measure up is driving all my outer-cup focus.

My kids would hardly know me if I wasn't on a diet of some sort— though they've learned to laugh with me about starting over on Monday so I can indulge in brownies today. I'm not especially glamorous, so you might not think of me as someone who obsesses over appearances, but I do. I spend far too much time worrying about how I measure up in the eyes of others. I spend far too much money on diet fads. And I spend far too many hours in dressing rooms, trying to track down clothes that will finally make my flaws disappear.

But these words of Jesus have me wondering. What if the outside of the cup doesn't matter nearly as much as I think? What if, dear sisters, our extra pounds aren't really the problem? What if our thinning hair, wrinkles, flabby arms, and bulging veins are just trivialities instead of the main issue? And what if our obsession with cleaning up the outside of the cup is actually evidence of some crusty, caked-on inner grime?

Jesus isn't telling us to stop caring for our appearance or looking our best on the outside. (We'll talk about our bodies' great worth in lesson 4.) But he is telling us to stop turning a blind eye to what's really going on inside.

Blind by Choice

Would you drink a lovely steaming latte after watching someone with the flu sneeze into it? No, but a blind woman would without knowing the difference—that is, until she started getting sick.

The Pharisees weren't physically blind; they were spiritually blind by choice. Their hearts were like bubbling cauldrons of greed and self-ishness, but they didn't care. The Pharisees rather enjoyed thinking of themselves as sinlessly clean and better than everyone else. And when Jesus got in their faces to point out their sin, it made them want to kill him—which in turn made Satan grin.

The Pharisees had excused God from his throne and now they were the ones sitting on thrones and pronouncing others "clean" or "unclean." But they were blind to their own filth, and Jesus—the true King—wanted to open their eyes and show them how to *truly* be clean.

Come with me back to the Pharisee's table and to the temple courts that Tuesday morning before Jesus died. Let's listen carefully to both accounts and glean from Jesus's instructions on how to go from blind-and-grimy to clean-and-free:

1. Have a Maker Makeover

Jesus said to his Pharisee dinner host, "Did not he who made the outside make the inside also?" (Luke 11:40). Our Maker created us as whole people, with no separation between our inner half and outer half. So when we give ourselves an outer-half makeover while neglecting our hearts, we deceive ourselves into thinking we're changed.

Suppose a woman who doesn't know Jesus and is stricken with insecurity comes to you for help. You show her how to improve her appearance and become more confident, but you never talk to her about Jesus or her sin. She might think she's been completely transformed, but she's only traded one problem for another. Her new confidence is in a brightened appearance, which will fade. Her new self-assurance is built on self, not God, and will quickly morph into pride or self-reliance. The fact is, **complete transformation involves the heart, which requires Jesus.**

My Maker wants to give me a makeover inside *and* out. He wants to scour away the jealousy, pride, and selfish ambition that have been causing my mirror-obsession in the first place.

2. Check for Greed

When Jesus talked about cleaning out the "inside of the cup," he mentioned the sin of greed specifically (Matt. 23:25).

Greed is never content. It always wants *more*. A greedy Comparison Girl doesn't want to be pretty; she wants to be the pretti*est*. She doesn't want the devoted eyes of just one man; she wants to draw the eyes of *all* men. She wants eye-turning power and fear-coating acceptance. She wants to look in the mirror and into the approving eyes of others and know that yes—finally—she measures up. Yet no matter how much approval she garners with her fresh, outer-cup glow, her inner greed is never satisfied because that's the nature of greed.

Supermodel Cameron Russell says, "If you ever are wondering, 'If I have thinner thighs and shinier hair, will I be happier?' you just need to meet a group of models, because they have the thinnest thighs, the shiniest hair, and the coolest clothes, and they're the most physically insecure women probably on the planet."[4]

If I have a greedy, unsatiated desire for approval, I'm foolish to think that losing ten pounds or getting eyelash extensions will help. I'll need to clean out the greed to be free.

3. Check for Self-Indulgence

Jesus mentioned self-indulgence specifically too (Matt. 23:25). Self-indulgence is giving in to *self*. For the woman obsessed with having a measure-up appearance, this is an easy habit to fall into. Whether it's products, treatments, apparel, or procedures, if it can improve her appearance, she *has* to have it. And often self-indulgence is cumulative.

I've noticed that the more I shop for clothes, the more I *want* to shop for clothes. The more I spend on makeup, the more I *need* to spend on makeup. The more frantic I become about weight gain, the more *obsessed* I become with dieting (which only makes me want to indulge in an ice cream sundae). If I constantly cave in to my have-to-have-it whims, I'm foolish to think that one more indulgence will not simply lead to another. I have to say *no* to myself and yes to God in order to clean out self-indulgence and be free.

4. Be Generous

Jesus gave a specific clean-up instruction to the Pharisee who had invited him to dinner: "But now as for what is inside you—be generous to the poor, and everything will be clean for you" (Luke 11:41 NIV). Jesus wasn't saying that generosity can cancel out our sin; only God can purge us on the inside and make us clean (Ps. 51:7). But we are fools to scrub away at the outer cup when the inside is what's filthy. Like the Pharisee, Jesus invites us to participate in our own inner-cup cleansing.

The Pharisee at the table might have clean hands, but he apparently also had money-greed issues. Jesus was handing him some cleanser that works on greed of all sorts: *Tip your measuring cup and start pouring. Think about someone other than yourself. Give something away.*

Greed grows on the inside. A greedy Comparison Girl is often oblivious to the me-focus that's gunking up her heart because she's too busy looking in the mirror. She keeps her outer shell scrubbed sparkly clean, while inside she's a selfish, grimy mess. She spends her life grabbing, not giving.

But here's the thing about measuring cups. **You can't be selfishly filling your cup and selflessly emptying it out at the same time.** That's why generous pouring serves as a cleanser for inner greed and self-indulgence. Why not try it out yourself? If you have style-greed, try giving away several of your favorite outfits or accent pieces. If you have attention-greed, try lavishing a baby with attention in the church nursery. If you have affirmation-greed, try texting hand-picked encouragement verses to several friends and family members. If you have approval-greed, try investing in an insecure teen.

When I catch myself comparing and obsessing about my skin-deep packaging, the best thing I can do is follow Jesus's clean-up instructions and find a way to be generous or activate my "spout." Just last week, I saw a woman at church whom I know casually. From across the atrium, I noticed her thin frame silhouetted by a trendy outfit. Seeing her made me feel rather frumpy and plain, but then I caught myself and asked, *How can I be generous today? How can I pour myself out?* So I walked over, greeted her, then followed up on a past conversation. She smiled, obviously pleased that I had sought her out. As we talked, I noticed again how pretty she was—only this time, instead of comparing, I was celebrating God's artistry in her. As we parted, she gave me a hug and said, "I appreciate you so much!" And I felt the same.

When I shift from comparing myself to celebrating others, from shifting my focus from the lines to the spout, it not only blesses my friends, it changes *me*. This is true at home, in my neighborhood, at church, and online. Each time I tip my measuring cup with self-forgetfulness, the lines become irrelevant . . . and a little more grime gets scrubbed from inside of my cup.

SET FREE

After years of food addiction, Rachel was invited to a Bible study. She didn't really think God could fix her, but she decided to give it a try. As Rachel began to study the truth of God's word for herself, she got her eyes *off* herself. *Maybe I've just been way too focused on me*, she thought.

One night, driving home from Bible study, Rachel realized that bigger than her struggle with food was her struggle with *sin*. Her endless greed for measure-up approval was never going away. And by turning to herself, she had turned from God. The thought grieved her very much.

There in the car, Rachel shared tears of regret and repentance with the Lord and felt forgiveness wash over her. As she pulled into her driveway, the garage door lifted, and so did the burden of her addiction. Miraculously, after fifteen years Rachel was set free. Today, as Rachel grows in her new security, freedom, and joy, she still acknowledges the pressure to be good-looking. But she says, "More than being pretty, I now want to be a beautiful person, a beautiful friend."

Is there some inner-cup struggle causing you to burden yourself with an extreme outer-cup agenda? Perhaps with Rachel you could say, *Maybe I've just been too focused on me.* Jesus wants to wash you with his truth and free you to be the beautiful person he created you to be.

≈ Read 1 Samuel 16:6–7. What does God look on and not look on? How does this concept reframe your struggle with comparing appearances?

≈ Reread Matthew 23:25–26. What evidences do you see of the following "inner cup" issues in your life? List any specific "outer cup"

extremes (like dieting, spending, social media behavior, etc.) that are caused by one or more of the following:
- approval greed
- popularity greed
- power greed (especially power over men)
- self-indulgence
- self-focus

How is the Spirit inviting you to participate in being cleansed from the inside out?

≈ Read 1 Peter 3:3–4 and list everything you learn about internal beauty. What is one way you will adorn yourself with inward beauty this week?

For Meditation: Matthew 23:26

First clean the inside of the cup and the plate, that the outside also may be clean.

The more overfocused I am on my outer cup, the more blind I am to the inner grime *causing* my outer focus. Jesus invites me to participate in washing my inner cup clean by generously pouring myself out. *Lord, show me the ways I've been too focused on me.*

Lesson 4: Whitewashed Tombs
Read Matthew 23:25–28 and Mark 5:1–20

I GRIMACED WHEN I saw the group photo someone posted. There I was in the middle, surrounded by tall, sophisticated, gorgeous women. Compared to them, I looked short and chunky.

I stared for a long time, loathing the photo. *Why didn't I choose to stand next to other short people?* Then I loathed the other women. *Why do they have to be so beautiful?* Then I loathed myself. *Why, oh why, am I so ugly?*

It had been a lovely event spent with women I love—some of them my dearest and most supportive friends. We had connected deeply, which was refreshing and fulfilling. But now the whole memory was tarnished with thoughts like: *Is that what I looked like the whole night? How disgusting.*

Comparisons like these expose the sin in my heart. Yes, *sin*.

Imagine the beautiful woman to my left sharing this photo on Facebook, saying, "Look how much prettier I am!" It wouldn't be hard to spot her sinful pride, right? And while it seems harsher to call my reaction pride, that's what it is. I'm just *wishing* that I could be the prettier one and loathing the fact that I'm not.

Satan doesn't care which form of pride I respond to group photos with—the self-loathing or self-exalting type. He just wants me to keep caving in to my own selfishness, measuring myself against others, and slipping back into comparison bondage. But God, who loves me, uses things like group photos to develop my humility. Each time I'm confronted with my flaws in a photo, in the mirror, or on the scale, it's a new opportunity to humble myself and say, "God, I trust you. You see me as your treasure, and I trust your eyes more than mine or anyone else's."

WHITEWASHED TOMBS

The scribes and Pharisees were preoccupied with looking great in each other's eyes, yet they had no regard for how they looked in God's eyes. So that Tuesday morning, with his time coming to a close, Jesus continued his intervention by adding one more woe to his list. This one surely got their attention:

> Woe to you, scribes and Pharisees, hypocrites! For you are like whitewashed tombs, which outwardly appear beautiful, but within are full of dead people's bones and all uncleanness. (Matt. 23:27)

You and I might visit cemeteries, but the Jews never did. As Jesus pointed out, tombs were full of dead people's bones. According to the law, if you touched a dead body, you were unclean and you'd have to follow the purification steps to become clean. Because of this, the Jews thought of tombs the way you and I might think of a sewer. So comparing a Pharisee to a tomb with whitewash would be like me comparing you to a sewer with a shiny new manhole cover. It wasn't a compliment.

Each year in early spring, just before Passover, the religious leaders would put a fresh coat of whitewash on the graves so visitors wouldn't mistakenly venture near and contaminate themselves (Num. 19:11).[5] The tombs looked beautiful from a distance, glimmering in the sunlight, but everyone knew that just inches below the surface were all things dead and unclean. The outside didn't match the inside.

Our way of "whitewashing" might look different from that of these religious leaders, but this imagery offers a somber warning to Comparison Girls who long to look beautiful from a distance.

Tomb Dwellers

The Bible only tells one story about a man who felt comfortable with tombs. He was a madman filled with unclean spirits, and he lived in a cemetery. Night and day he wandered among the tombs, crying out and cutting himself.

When Jesus showed up, he ordered the man's demons to leave him and go into a herd of pigs. The herd then rushed down an embankment and drowned. The man, no longer a threat to himself or others, miraculously reentered civilization and told everyone what Jesus had done for him (Mark 5:1–20).

As with this madman, preoccupation with death is a sure mark of the enemy's influence in our lives. Suicide, cutting, and self-harm seem to be Satan's favorite suggestions lately. But before we'll even consider these death-inspired behaviors, he must first taunt us with shame and convince us we're worthless. He loves to haunt our cemetery-hearts with echoes from the past, messages first spoken by people but repeated by the enemy. *You'll never be good enough. You're not worth it. You're a disaster. They wish you were gone.* Some of the messages that hurt most deeply have to do with our skin-deep appearance. *You're ugly. You're so fat. Who could ever find you desirable?*

The best thing we could possibly do is run for help, invite truth in, and examine these taunts in the light. But often we do the opposite. We whitewash our flaws and our pain. We project confidence by layering style and personality overtop our sense of worthlessness. We button crisp white sleeves over the places we've torn our own skin. We paint on a smile to divert attention from our aching inadequacies. We even exude vibrancy and life, but inside, we're still living among the tombstones.

Are you someone who has tried to whitewash your sense of worthlessness? Or maybe you're more like the Pharisees, whitewashing your corruption and pride? Either way, whether you're hiding an inflated or deflated view of yourself, Satan will keep handing you the paintbrush of hypocrisy, saying, "You can't let anyone see."

MAINTAINING THE PERIMETER

The whole reason for the whitewash was to keep people from venturing too close to the tombs. Ours serves the same purpose. We don't whitewash to draw people close; we're trying to keep them away. Away from our shameful imperfections and inadequacies. We want to be seen as perfect.

This is why we take 116 selfies, then post the most flattering one, taken at just the right angle to disguise flaws and enhance beauty. This is also why, after posting the perfect photo, we pull the real us—the us with the muffin top and wrinkles and dark circles under our eyes—back into isolation. We're most comfortable when we can maintain the perimeter. We'd rather have friends like or comment on our whitewashed photo than invite them over, where they might see our deficiencies up close.

Since Satan masquerades as an angel of light (2 Cor. 11:14), it's no surprise that he tempts us to adopt the same whitewashing strategy. And in our pride and self-sufficiency, we agree. Vulnerability should be avoided at all costs. We have to maintain the perimeter. We have to keep whitewashing and looking beautiful from a distance. Because **what would happen if the truth about us were known?**

A POSTED SCORE

Though my friend Raeanne loved her training as a competitive gymnast, there was one day each month that she dreaded: the day the coaches posted each gymnast's name and weight on the gym wall, where it would stay for the following month.

Raeanne's weight was always healthy and normal, but her good friend Katie always came in at about eight pounds less. Nobody pointed out that Katie was three inches shorter and more petite. So Raeanne was left to compare and draw her own conclusions, which led to her distorted body image, view of food, and sense of self-worth.

You and I don't likely worry about our weight being posted publicly (the very thought gives me heart palpitations), but we *do* live in a measure-up world that is constantly taking skin-deep assessments. Nobody explains that **it's healthy and normal to look different from our friends, our sisters, our neighbors, or even ourselves . . . ten years ago.** We're left to compare and come to our own conclusions. We live in fear, worried that any moment someone is going to post our score and validate our greatest fear: we didn't measure up after all.

A DIM MIRROR

We tend to "score" ourselves one of two ways. Like the Pharisees, we compare and give ourselves high, self-inflating scores, which rot our hearts with pride. Or, like the man cutting himself in the cemetery, we withdraw and give ourselves low, self-depreciating scores, which decay our hearts with shame. Either way, we keep whitewashing our secret selves and maintaining the perimeter, afraid of being discovered.

This, my friend, is the work of the enemy. The truth is, our worth is not open for evaluation. God, our Creator, has meticulously crafted each of our bodies and stamped us with his image. Ephesians 2:10 says we are his workmanship—his unique masterpieces. This is God's assessment, and his holy, penetrating eyes are the ones that matter. Today we only see ourselves in a dimly lit mirror (1 Cor. 13:12), but God sees his original design. There is coming a day when he will remove the corrosive, dimming effects of the curse and restore our original luster.

Nancy DeMoss Wolgemuth writes, "It's conceivable that someone who didn't recognize or appreciate fine art would toss a masterpiece into the trash. Would that make the painting any less valuable? Not at all. The true worth of the art would be seen when an art collector spotted the painting and said, 'That is a priceless piece, and I am willing to pay any amount to acquire it.'"[6] This, dear sister, is what God has said about you.

Satan roams the earth trying to capture God's masterpieces (you and me) and throw us in the trash, causing us to conclude that we're worthless garbage. But God was willing to pay the highest ransom—the death of Jesus, his Son—just to redeem us. *That's* what we are worth.

A RESTORING KING

Some people like to say, "You're enough, just as you are," but that's not really true. We *aren't* enough. The dirt and grime of sin have left us in a diminished state. Our eternal bodies are eaten alive by death. Our resemblance of the Father is tarnished and dim.

So here are our choices. We can keep whitewashing over the rotting decay and trying to project confidence and perfection. Or we can let Jesus inside to begin his curse-reversing restoration.

The Pharisees were still choosing the whitewash. There at the temple, just three days before his death and after three years of sharing the way of life, Jesus told them, "Outwardly [you] appear righteous to others, but within you are full of hypocrisy and lawlessness" (Matt. 23:28). It was a jolting and harsh rebuke to ones who looked so perfect from a distance. But if they were ever to become truly clean and beautiful on the inside—not just a whitewashed facade—they needed to humble themselves and throw open their tombstone-sealed hearts to their truth-telling King.

CLEAN AND BEAUTIFUL

Here's the amazing thing about Jesus—nothing makes him unclean. When he touched unclean people or came in contact with unclean spirits, he was unaffected by them, yet they were drastically affected by him. He made the unclean things *clean.*

Jesus refuses to maintain the perimeter; there is no need. So he comes near and knocks. When we humble ourselves, we unlock whitewashed doors and open our lives to him, Jesus comes in and makes us clean. Our Jesus spills light into every nook and cranny of our shadowy hearts, exposing the lies and bringing truth and life.

For far too long the messages of the hissing snake from Eden's lost garden have been echoing forward and infiltrating our lives with death. But our Jesus has come to speak life over us with a conquering lion's roar.

The snake says *she's worthlessss.* Jesus says SHE'S PRICELESS.

The snake says *she's ssscum.* Jesus says SHE'S CHOSEN.

The snake says *she's hideoussss.* Jesus says SHE'S BEAUTIFUL!

Comparison Girl, whatever story of pride or worthlessness you're telling about yourself, Jesus—our restoring King—tells a better one. Is there some tombstone you need Jesus to push back? Is there a dark corner of shame you need him to enter? Is there some dead, rotting memory you need him to touch with his light? Is there a trash-talking voice from the past you need him to silence with his roar?

Jesus came to make each of us beautiful and clean. Because of him, we can all stop whitewashing and stop maintaining our perimeters. As we move toward each other in vulnerability, our flaws are exposed, but there is no risk because God sees the masterpieces that we really are, and his eyes matter most.

≈ Read Mark 5:1–20 and contrast Satan's effect and Jesus's effect on the man's life. What parallels do you see in your life?

≈ Read Matthew 23:27–28. What are the ways you "whitewash" over what's really going on and maintain a perimeter? Are you more prone to self-exalting or self-loathing pride? How does your pride keep you from being vulnerable?

≈ Read 1 Peter 2:4. Who determined that Jesus was worthless? Who determined that he was precious and had great worth? Answer the same questions about yourself.

≈ Read Hebrews 12:2. How did Jesus feel about his shame? What did he look forward to? How can you do the same?

≈ Read Matthew 4:16. How does this verse describe your life "among the tombs" before coming to Jesus and "in the light" afterward?

For Meditation: Matthew 4:16

> For those dwelling in the region and shadow of death,
> on them a light has dawned.

In pride, I "whitewash" so I'll look beautiful from a distance. In humility, I let go of the perimeter. *Jesus, thank you for coming near and making me clean. I will trust your eyes instead of my own to determine my worth.*

Chapter Five

Comparing Our Ministries

I SAW A video on Twitter of a cute little girl who must have been about two being introduced to her newborn baby brother. Her parents gently tucked him in her lap and sweetly urged her to admire the baby, saying, "Ella, can you give him a kiss?"

Ella was not impressed. She hilariously looked straight ahead with arms limp and her expression grim. At one point she glanced down at the adorable little bundle in her lap, but only with grumpy skepticism.

Ella's grim expression (minus the cuteness) reminds me of how a women's ministry director looks when some new ministry pops up down the street. Or how a seasoned church leader looks when some new, fresh-faced leader is getting all the attention. Or how a Bible study coordinator looks when some new study is stealing all her group members.

It is the world and Satan (not the church) suggesting that in order to *be* somebody, we have to outdo somebody. But it's not just the people out in the world being influenced. When James 3:16 says, "For wherever there is jealousy and selfish ambition, there you will find disorder and evil of every kind" (NLT), the "wherever" includes the church.

Up until now, we've been glancing back and forth between comparison in the world and in the church, but for this chapter we'll focus exclusively on Christians laboring side by side in ministry. We might *think* that because we're disciples who serve, we are immune to our enemy's tactics, but Satan knows we aren't. Some of his most effective comparison traps are laid within our women's ministry teams, church small groups, and Bible studies—which makes this conversation about comparing our ministries one of our most important yet.

Lesson 1: Expecting More
Read Matthew 19:27–20:16

JESUS DIDN'T SHARE the vineyard parable as a stand-alone story. It was part of a longer conversation with his disciples—one we talked about at length in chapter three. Remember when the rich man walked away and Peter asked, "See, we have left everything and followed you. What then will we have?" (Matt. 19:27).

Jesus encouraged Peter and the other disciples to dream big about kingdom rewards. He said that everyone who leaves something behind for his sake "will receive a hundredfold and will inherit eternal life. *But* many who are first will be last, and the last first" (Matt. 19:29–30, emphasis added). Notice how, with the word "but," Jesus switches gears from encouragement to warning? That's where we'll pick up our study today.

Jesus's response reminds me of the instructions that I used to give to my kids on the bike path. "You can go up ahead, *but* when you get to the road you have to stop. Do you hear me? You have to *stop* at the road."

Peter wasn't just asking whether kingdom workers get rewarded. He wanted to know if those who live by the spout and pour *more* or pour *faster* or pour *sooner* than others are the ones who are considered *greater*. And Jesus, seeing the heart behind Peter's question, encouraged him to pedal hard toward heaven's rewards but then brake hard before crossing into the me-focused pride of trying to be "first."

This exchange between Peter and Jesus provides the backdrop for Jesus's story about the vineyard workers.

A STORY OF A VINEYARD

The story goes like this. A master goes out before 6 a.m. (the beginning of the workday[1]) to hire workers for his vineyard. After the master agrees to pay them a generous wage for the day, some workers enter the vineyard and eagerly get to work. But then the master does something unexpected. He returns at 9 a.m. to call more workers. This time he says he'll pay them "whatever is right." The same thing happens again at 12 p.m. and 3 p.m. Then the master goes out once more at 5 p.m.—just an hour before the workday is over—and hires yet another group of workers.

At the end of the day, even though the workers all clocked in at different times, they're each paid the same generous wage. The 5 p.m. workers were thrilled, but the 6 a.m. workers were frustrated. It's true that they received exactly the agreed upon amount, yet "they thought they would receive more" (Matt. 20:10).

As we will see, Jesus built this story around the 6 a.m. workers' frustration, which was based on two things: comparison and expectations. Compared to the others, they had worked more. They had toiled under the scorching sun as the other workers sat in the shade. They had carried the burden of a full day's work. No one else; only them. Because of this, they had an underlying expectation: they worked more, so they should *receive* more.

But the upside-down kingdom is not a place to work hard, get ahead, and come in first. That's the way the world operates. **The upside-down kingdom is a place to serve.**

Servants aren't the ones straining to be recognized. And those seeking recognition are not servants. This is easy to acknowledge but much harder to live—especially when you're the one who worked harder than anyone else, under the summer heat.

6 A.M. WORKERS

I was raised in a home where it was normal to be at church working. My dad was a deacon and taught Sunday school for decades. My mom prepared homemade Wednesday evening meals for our entire church family. You could always find the Berrys serving at church. It's what we did. We *wanted* to be there, ministering among God's people.

It's probably because of my "6 a.m.-worker" heritage that some comparison traps are easier for me to sidestep. I can shrug off not being as wealthy or beautiful, or not having career success like other women. I can plug my ears when the world says these are the measure-up ways to find validation and worth. Yet this same measure-up validation and worth is what I go looking for as I put on my worker name badge inside the church. I don't like to admit this, but I crave affirmation in ministry. I long for church people to say, "She's such a servant. She does so much work for God."

Now, as we learned in chapter one, it's good for me to bring the unique gifts that God has placed in my hands and share them smorgasbord-style with the church. It's right for me to find purpose and belonging among God's people as I serve. But when my ambition is to be lifted up as a standout servant, that's when I need to check for measure-up pride.

Are you the type of volunteer who might bankrupt your church if you were paid for all your "overtime" hours? Are you the one who comes to everyone's mind when they think of a "servant" at church? Are you the first one to arrive? Are you the last one to leave? Have you been there the longest? Then join me, dear sister, in receiving this warning from Jesus.

As the daughter of 6 a.m. workers, I can speak on some authority when I say that those of us who tip our measuring cups to the extreme and serve Jesus with reckless abandon are at greater risk of pedaling full steam into measure-up pride. Right there in the middle of the church kitchen, the Bible study rooms, or the nursery, our me-focused hearts tempt us to look around and compare all that we've done with all they haven't. And to conclude that we deserve *more*. More recognition. More appreciation. More validation. More praise. More honor. More loyalty.

We'd never name these expectations, of course. And sometimes we're not even aware of them. That is, until we *don't* get the "more" we thought we deserved. That's when we realize we've stepped right into another comparison trap.

I've noticed that God rarely reveals my me-focused pride when I'm receiving the validation and affirmation I crave. I simply see myself as a servant of the Lord—pedaling on ahead of all the rest. But then comes that moment when I'm not acknowledged for doing more or I'm not praised for serving longest. It's always hurtful when your work is overlooked or undervalued, but for a 6 a.m. worker it's absolutely wounding.

These wounds of unmet expectations are what Trish—a devoted servant of the Lord—experienced recently.

A Bitter Root

Matt and Trish entered church ministry with sheer excitement. Matt held the "associate pastor" title, but Trish was equally committed. For several years they served side by side, pouring everything into their church. Then unexpectedly, under new leadership and after a reorganization, Matt was edged out. He was hurt and discouraged, but far more so after he learned—in an interview—that his former boss had given him a poor review, saying, "I'd never hire him."

Matt and Trish felt deeply betrayed, both by this pastor and by God. They had invested everything. They'd built relationships and sacrificed greatly. Why were they being rejected? At thirty-three years old, Trish longed to move into a bigger house and grow her family like many of her friends were. Instead, she was moving to a small apartment in a new town and working nights while her husband tried to reset his career. Trish could feel the seeds of bitterness sprouting. *Is this how Jesus treats those who sacrifice the most?*

Six a.m. workers often set out like Matt and Trish did—with high hopes of being used by God and producing fruit for the kingdom. Then when our sacrifice and hard work are met with rejection or betrayal, the poisonous roots of bitterness sprout involuntarily in our hearts. But Hebrews 12:15 warns, "Watch out that no poisonous root of bitterness grows up to trouble you, corrupting many" (NLT).

When we're wounded, we should look to Jesus, who also was hurt, rejected, and betrayed by his own people—God's people. Yet on the cross when Jesus was offered bitter wine mixed with poison, he refused to drink it (Matt. 27:34). Drinking deeply of bitterness by rehearsing our resentments always promises to be satisfying, but bitterness is poison. Like Jesus, we must turn our face and refuse it.[2]

Hebrews 12 not only warns against bitterness, it also reminds us that God disciplines the ones he loves—not in a punishing way, but in a Fatherly way. Discipline is never pleasant; it's always painful. But in the end it produces good *fruit* (Heb. 12:6–11).

In the vineyard, fruit is what we're after, right? But fruit takes time. Often it's not till much later that we realize God *was* producing fruit, which would've remained dormant if not for the painful discipline he asked us to endure. As 6 a.m. workers looking for extra validation, we sometimes find that God uses our unmet expectations to reveal the measure-up pride that has been holding us back in the vineyard. Our wounded pride is meant not to hurt us but to produce more fruit (Heb. 12:11).

Remember that it was Peter's question that prompted this parable in the first place. Peter was asking whether workers who pour *more, faster,* or *sooner* than others are the ones who are considered *greater.* Do you see how Peter's measure-up agenda could have made him less fruitful in God's work? Jesus did. It was the point of his vineyard story. Comparison Girl, if you haven't received the "more" you were expecting, don't recoil in bitterness or betrayal. Invite your Lord to use your wounded pride to make you even more fruitful for him.

QUIET FRUIT

After their move, Trish was pretty resentful. The temptation to sip bitterness's poison was great. Her work at her former church had been so meaningful and significant, but this new town was notorious for being filled with Christian workers. *My gifts will never be used here,* Trish thought. But she was wrong.

In her desire to learn what God wanted to teach her, Trish leaned hard into Bible study that year. She worked nights on a hospital floor that often didn't have much for her to do, so sometimes Trish would pull out her Bible. One night Trish's coworker Mary asked what she was reading. This sparked a four-hour conversation, with Mary asking question after question about God.

In all of Trish's church ministry years, she had never experienced anything like this. God *was* using her! He *did* have a plan! By God's choice, not hers, Trish had gone from being a 6 a.m. worker with great expectations to being a 5 p.m. worker who assumed she'd never produce anything of kingdom worth. Yet in a quiet hospital wing, in the middle of the night, God had used Trish to bring good news to a woman with no purpose or joy. In both of their lives, God was quietly producing fruit.

Friend, as we tip our measuring cups and work hard for the kingdom, may it not be for recognition or to get ahead. And when our pride is wounded, may we refuse to drink the poison of bitterness. Instead, let's be joyful workers who quietly anticipate more fruit.

≈ Which workers from Matthew 20:1–7 best represent you? Why?

≈ Matthew 20:10 says the 6 a.m. workers "thought they would receive more." Journal about any situations in which you have craved or expected more recognition, more appreciation, more validation, more praise, more honor, or more loyalty. Lay down each of these expectations before the Lord, refusing to fall into a comparison trap.

≈ Read Hebrews 12:11–17. In verse 11, what does Fatherly discipline yield? In verse 17, what does bitterness yield? How have both of these been true in your life?

≈ When has your work gone undervalued or overlooked? How does your woundedness correlate with an expectation for validation or honor? Keep Hebrews 12:11 handy on a notecard or on your phone as truth to turn to as you refuse to drink from the "bitter cup."

For Meditation: Hebrews 12:11 (NIV)

No discipline seems pleasant at the time, but painful. Later on, however, it produces a harvest of righteousness and peace for those who have been trained by it.

Especially when I've worked the longest or hardest, I must watch for measure-up comparison traps in the church. Striving for more recognition or validation is not the way of the kingdom. *Lord, I will turn my face from the cup of bitterness and humbly anticipate spiritual fruit.*

Lesson 2: Lumped In as Equals
Read Matthew 20:1–16

"WHERE'S ALICE?" I asked. I had been told that Alice and I would be ministry partners this year. "Oh, Alice is helping out with Jan's team," someone responded, and instantly I knew. Alice was being groomed to move up in leadership. And I was being left behind.

Why wasn't I chosen? I wondered. *Why is Alice being given this role instead of me?* I didn't want this to bother me. I tried not to feel hurt or insecure, but jealousy sprung up in my heart anyway.

In God's kingdom, where we celebrate each other's unique callings, gifts, and assignments, I find it easy to cheer for those who serve in ways that I never could. I find it thrilling to encourage those that I'm ministering to. But the sister whose gifts are like mine and who does what I do? She's the one I'm often tempted to be jealous of and compare myself with. I look at the grapes in her basket and measure her vineyard work against mine. When she's chosen first, I ask, *Why her, God? Why not me?*

AMPLIFIED INEQUALITY

What if Jesus told the story of the vineyard workers this way?

> The kingdom of heaven is like a master of a house who went out at daybreak and hired all the workers he needed for his vineyard. Then all the workers worked a full day, and they all received the same generous wage.

It isn't much of a plotline, right? By telling the story with workers starting at various times, Jesus purposefully emphasizes the disparity between how much the workers accomplished. And then Jesus adds one more story detail which amplifies the inequality even more. The last vineyard workers—the ones who started at 5 p.m.—are the ones paid first.

If the 6 a.m. workers were paid first, they would have gone on their merry way, right? They wouldn't have even known that the others received the same wage. But because the last were paid first, the 6 a.m. workers stood watching while the other groups received equal pay. Jesus further draws our attention to this order-of-payment detail by bracketing the story with two red-letter comparisons.

***

Red-Letter Comparisons: "But many who are first will be last, and the last first" (Matt. 19:30).
"So the last will be first, and the first last" (Matt. 20:16).

***

It's as if Jesus shines a spotlight on the expressions of the workers as they receive their pay. The 5 p.m. workers, or "lasts," are astonished and overjoyed! They only worked an easy hour and can't believe the generosity of the master. But the 6 a.m. "firsts" are outraged—after twelve hours' work—over their mistreatment. They grumble at the master through clenched teeth, saying, "You have made them equal to us!" (Matt. 20:12). And as Comparison Girls, you and I look on, thinking, "Well, I kind of agree."

BEING LUMPED IN

If my child gave a Mother's Day card to some other mom, that wouldn't sit well with me. If the university I graduated from started giving away diplomas for half the credits, I would be angry. If someone else's name was added beside mine on the front of this book, I would be frustrated. I might be tempted to call the publisher and say, "You have made her equal to me!"

We naturally believe things should be fair. Honor and recognition should be deserved. And when those less worthy are given equal honor and recognition, we feel *dishonored* and *unrecognized*. This is particularly true in the church.

When we serve in ministry, we aren't just doing work. These are our gifts to God that we're pouring onto the altar. We want God to notice what we've given, especially when we've given *more*. And when there's someone who hasn't served as long, or whose gifts seem less worthy, or whose sacrifice seems minimal compared with ours, it's bothersome to be lumped in together . . . especially as Comparison Girls.

We probably wouldn't argue against God giving someone the same eternal life that he's given us. And we don't get upset about heavenly rewards either, since we can't see those. What bothers us are the get-ahead rewards in the here and now. Like when somebody serves God less, yet she becomes wealthy or gets promoted, engaged, or honored. That's what gets under our skin. Along with the 6 a.m. workers—mad because they got the same wage as everybody else—we cry, "You have made her *equal* to me!"

But in saying so, we reveal three wrong assumptions we're making about the kingdom of heaven.

Wrong Assumption 1: Greatness Is Obvious

The great ones of heaven may not be obvious to us here on earth since we're so accustomed to the world's way of comparing. As in the close of the vineyard story, there will be some surprises in heaven. Remember Jesus's red-letter comparison? "Many who are first will be last, and the last first" (Matt. 19:30).

There are some of us who think of ourselves as "firsts" among God's people and demand to be recognized for our longtime service and superior contributions to kingdom work. As we lift ourselves up, we show we are actually "lasts" in the kingdom, because God opposes the proud (1 Peter 5:5). There are others of us who think of ourselves as "lasts" and consider others far more qualified to serve in kingdom work. We are unimpressed with ourselves and chuckle at the thought that God would even use one like us. Our willingness to serve in quiet anonymity shows we are actually "firsts," because God exalts the humble (1 Peter 5:6).

Wrong Assumption 2: Adapting to Our Circumstances Eliminates Jealousy

We might be tempted to think, "If the workers in the story were paid in the opposite order, there wouldn't be a problem." But it's not true. The problem of jealous comparison and superiority was there all along. The order-of-payment detail only gave rise to it. Suppose I am jealous today and see no reason to be grateful. Even if my circumstance changes tomorrow, my attitude won't. Because the circumstances aren't the problem.

I remember looking longingly at the beautiful way a husband and wife in our church led a ministry together. It was like a graceful dance, and I was so jealous! *If only my husband and I could be like that couple.* But when I brought it up, my husband reminded me of his demanding season at work. He said he only had capacity for his every-other-week ministry to our church's two-year-olds. Well, this made me mad. I told myself that if we could do ministry together like that other couple, I wouldn't be jealous at all. But the truth is, I had no reason to be jealous. God was blessing both my husband and me as we served him in different ways. And if I *were* in that other wife's shoes, I'd only find some other reason to be jealous. Jealousy doesn't stem from the situation I'm in; it stems from my heart.[3]

Wrong Assumption 3: The Kingdom Is Marked by Equality

The *in*equality of the kingdom is the whole point of this parable. People who worked an hour got paid the same as those who worked twelve. The story corrects the idea that we can work hard, do more, and get ahead—which is rooted in the measure-up, selfish ambition of the world. There's a reason that Isaiah compares our righteousness to filthy rags (Isa. 64:6 NIV).

There's no use in keeping record of how many hours we've worked or how much we've accomplished for the kingdom, since we've all fallen dreadfully short of being worthy (Rom. 3:23). And when we stamp our foot demanding the honor we deserve, it's clear that we've forgotten what we actually *do* deserve: "The wages of sin is death" (Rom. 6:23).

In the story, the generous wage represents eternal life, and none of us deserve to receive it.

NOT A THING TO BE GRASPED

So how should we—the undeserving citizens of the kingdom of heaven—react when someone even less deserving is lifted up? What should we say when our contributions are overlooked? What should we do when things seem unfair or unequal or unjust?

Let's consider Jesus's responses to these very challenges. Underline and add an ≠ sign over any parts of this verse which depict unfairness, inequality, or injustice in comparison with what Jesus deserved.

"Have this mind among yourselves, which is yours in

Christ Jesus, who, though he was in the form of God,

did not count equality with God a thing to be grasped,

but emptied himself, by taking the form of a servant,

being born in the likeness of men. And being found in

human form, he humbled himself by becoming obe-

dient to the point of death, even death on a cross."

Philippians 2:5–8

Even though Jesus never stopped *being* God, he didn't cling to his equality with God. He didn't consider it "a thing to be grasped." Jesus didn't grip tighter to equal status when it seemed to slip. He was content to *not* be equal—to submit and say, "Not my will," even when God allowed him to die.

Jesus took his measuring cup and flipped it upside down. **Jesus emptied himself and became a servant. He poured everything out on the cross so that we might be lifted from our depravity.** He was mocked, tortured, and spat upon so that he could bring us from death to eternal life.

How inappropriate, then, to keep a ledger, comparing what we've poured from our measuring cups with what others are pouring. How silly to track everyone's contributions. How ridiculous to pound our fists on the table and demand fairness and equality—as the recipients of such extravagant generosity.

ROOTING FOR MY SISTERS

After a few months, my suspicions about Alice were confirmed when I received an email announcing her new leadership position. I read it on a Monday morning, still in bed—completely spent after speaking at a retreat. Immediately a pang of jealousy shot through me, and I wanted to cry into my pillow. *Why her, God? Why not me?*

I felt compelled to get out my measuring stick and stack up all the evidence showing that I deserved this honor more than Alice did. I had served longer. I was more experienced. I was better than Alice at telling funny stories and getting people to like me. But then I also wanted to wallow in self-pity because of the many ways Alice is more gifted than me. She's certainly prettier. And she has way more followers on Instagram. And she teaches the Bible with such clarity.

Alice's honor made me feel *dishonored*. I wanted to groan, pull a pillow over my head, and avoid Alice from that day forward. But I recognized my inner Comparison Girl talking. I was thinking like a jealous 6 a.m. worker arguing for equality—which is not the way of the kingdom. Instead, Jesus wanted me to think like him and "do nothing out of rivalry or conceit, but in humility count Alice more significant than myself" (see Phil. 2:3).

When I picked up the phone to call Alice and cheer her on, instantly my heart filled with joy. I remembered how gifted Alice is, and I could see how her efforts would make the vineyard even more fruitful. But my heart also filled with relief, because in contrast with Alice's bubbly enthusiasm over her new role, I just wanted to take a nap. I love speaking at retreats, but I was weary. I had nothing left to give and Alice did—partly because she *hadn't* just spoken at a retreat. According to God's exact arrangement, Alice and I have different gifts. We're suited for different assignments. Why should I want hers when God has given me my own?

Sisters, the world urges us to clamor for equality and demand the recognition we deserve. But in Jesus's kingdom, things are different. Here, we cheer each other on with self-forgetful humility. Rather than groaning from under our pillows and avoiding each other, we lean *into* comparison, asking, "How is my assignment different from hers?"

Let's be me-free workers who root for each other and labor side by side, amazed by our collective good fortune. Can you believe it? We're the ones who have received eternal life!

≈ Who are you jealous of in ministry? Which of the three wrong assumptions are you making in this situation?
   • Wrong Assumption 1: Greatness is obvious.
   • Wrong Assumption 2: Adapting to our circumstances eliminates jealousy.
   • Wrong Assumption 3: The kingdom is marked by equality.

≈ Make a list of all the people that you work with in ministry. Write out 1 Peter 5:5b. Why do you think it says "all of you"? What is one way you can "get dressed" with humility each time you minister beside these other workers?

≈ Read 1 Peter 5:6–11.
   • How do you see the promise in 1 Peter 5:6 displayed in the vineyard story?
   • How are you currently putting verse 6 into practice?
   • How does waiting on God for recognition create anxiety? What does verse 7 say you should do with this anxiety? Why?
   • Why do Comparison Girls in ministry need to remember verse 8?

- What suffering have you faced in ministry? Why is it helpful to remember this is common (v. 9)?
- What word in verse 10 encourages you most?

For Meditation: 1 Peter 5:6

> Humble yourselves, therefore, under the mighty hand
> of God so that at the proper time he may exalt you.

When I stamp my foot and say, "You have made her equal to me!" it's clear I've forgotten what I *do* deserve—which is death, not eternal life. *Lord, I want to root for my fellow vineyard workers and humbly ask, "How is my assignment different from hers?"*

Lesson 3: Frustrated "Firsts"
Read Matthew 20:1–16

MY SON'S SCHOOL came up with a new fundraiser: auctioning front-row, VIP seating for the school musicals. At each performance, the lucky (and generous) winners get to sit in the comfy couches right up in front. They gave the most money. They get the best seats.

Sometimes we look to God for the same type of arrangement. We gave the most. We should be enjoying the comfy seats. That's what we hoped for, at least. But instead, we're in the last row on folding chairs while someone else is up front—with their growing ministry, thriving family, or life of comfort and ease. We think that we're frustrated with the person who's been blessed, but really we're mad at God.

Notice that when the workers say, "You have made them equal to us!" (Matt. 20:12), the "you" they are addressing is the master. It's a picture of the way we sometimes address God—grumbling because of his kindness to some other kingdom worker. We come to him with prayers like:

- God, why did she get the solo when I'm the one who's been on worship team for years?
- God, why was she asked to be a Bible study leader instead of me? I'm more gifted than she is!
- God, why is their son going into ministry and ours isn't even going to church? We're the ones who did family devotions each night!
- God, why did he choose to date her, not me? She's completely immature in her faith!
- God, why was I not given the role? I am way more serious about Bible study!
- God, why is her family together while mine is split apart? I'm the one who never cheated!

Each protest, whispered by a Comparison Girl and directed toward God, reveals a serious misunderstanding.

Mad at God

My friend Jill worked a job that paid about $12,000 per year to support her husband while he was going to seminary. There was no money for extras, but one year they used all their birthday and Christmas money to buy nice bikes—which would serve as both their exercise plan and their date-night entertainment. Then one afternoon they parked the bikes right outside their seminary apartment, and a few hours later the bikes were gone.

Jill was mad. "Really, God? After all we're sacrificing? After all we've given up to be here? Couldn't you have rerouted that thief to steal somebody else's bikes?"

Those of us who work hard in God's vineyard often keep a running tally in our minds. We think, "Here's what I gave to you, God. Now here's what I expect you to give to me." The formula seems tidy and logical. Yet **as we present our expectations, we act as though *we* are God, and he's the one who serves *us*.**

Friends, this is a serious breach of conduct for those who serve the most high God. As one commentator put it, "It is wicked to wrong God; but still worse to think oneself wronged by God."[4] The truth is, God doesn't answer to us any more than the master in the vineyard answered to his servants.

The master replied to those grumbling against him with three questions. And as God's servants, it would be good for us to consider these questions as well.

Question 1 from the Master: Didn't We Have an Agreement?

The workers agreed to be paid a specific, generous wage, and that's what they received. So what is our agreement, as God's vineyard workers?

One day our work will come to an end and we'll receive eternal life—not as a payment for work, since no work is required. And there are no contract clauses about extra benefits (like protection from bike thieves) for those who work harder or sacrifice more. God came to us not as a Master but as a Father longing for his children to come home. He offered us an eternal dwelling and we accepted. That is our agreement.

Question 2 from the Master: Am I Not Allowed to Do What I Choose?

God does not answer to us. He's the king of the kingdom, the master of the vineyard, and the owner of everything. And he can give whomever he likes whatever he pleases.

From the beginning in the garden, Satan's the one who has been suggesting we challenge God and question his goodness. But remember that this line of reasoning is what caused our eternal life to be sliced off with death. When we act as though God answers to us, we align ourselves with Satan—for he does the same thing. Whether we treat him as such or not, God *is* the King of the universe and the creator of all. He gets to choose what he'll give and to whom.

Question 3 from the Master: Do You Begrudge My Generosity?

Here's the literal translation for this question: "Is your eye evil?" An evil eye is always filled with jealousy. It looks over at a fellow worker with slack-jawed resentment, saying, "No fair, God! She hasn't worked nearly as hard in ministry as I have. Why are you rewarding her with *more?*"

More people. More responses. More growth. Each reward is a display of God's extravagant generosity. So my response, when the Master chooses to be particularly gracious to a co-laborer, should be to clap my hands in delighted worship! How unfitting when my eyes fill instead with begrudging resentment. How evil to look upon God's generosity with disgust.

SNATCHING THE SPOTLIGHT

Jesus's story contrasts two groups of workers: those who arrived at the vineyard last and those who arrived first. In his storytelling, Jesus casts the spotlight first on the 5 p.m. workers, who—in their astonishment and delight over being paid a full day's wage for an hour's work—are jumping up and down and hugging each other because of their good fortune. As we smile at their joy, our eyes naturally turn to find the master who has been so very generous. There he is, looking on and enjoying the scene just as much as we are. But after only a quick glance, our attention is diverted by the spotlight shifting to another group. It's the 6 a.m. workers, spewing their jealous anger.

This "spotlight snatch" is our enemy's aim in real life, every single time God displays his generosity.

Suppose God—who is free to be generous in any way he likes—chooses to reward my sister in ministry. She's a Christian author like me, but she's new. She hasn't worked nearly as hard or long as I have. Then on day one, her book begins to sell like hotcakes. The printers can hardly keep up, the demand is so high. Her writing ministry skyrockets overnight in a way that can't be explained simply by hard work. It's clear that God has been extravagantly generous.

One day, at an award assembly, I hear her name called to receive an award. But as I watch her walk onstage, I do not smile, jump up and down, or clap with excitement over God's generosity. Nor do I seek out the smiling face of God. My evil eye is too busy darting between her ministry rewards and mine. The discrepancy feels like mistreatment, and my Comparison Girl heart fills with such jealous resentment that I cannot sit still. With the spotlight still resting on her, I march out on center stage with my eyes flashing and demand, "God, why have you been kind to *her* and not to *me*?" And the moment I do so, Satan grins, for I have just snatched the spotlight from God and played into his scheme.

Friends, when God generously blesses someone else's ministry, it is his glory—not hers—that echoes like applause across the universe. And we, the ones looking on from the side, either multiply God's glory with our praise or stifle his glory with our begrudging protests.

We need to see rewards in ministry for what they truly are. When people turn to God, when spiritual fruit ripens, when a servant's platform expands because her audience is delighting in truth, all of these say little about the one on the platform and much about God. For any time that spiritual fruit multiplies, the kindness and generosity of God is on display! And who are we to begrudge such a thing?

It is with an evil eye that we look with jealousy at the co-laborer God is rewarding. And **not only does our evil-eyed jealousy stifle God's glory, it steals our own joy.**

ENVY-FREE JOY

Steve Bezner was a college student studying to be a pastor. He was a dedicated, 6 a.m.-type worker, yet God was blessing his roommate, Matt Chandler, instead. It all started when Matt (now pastor of the Village Church in Texas) was chosen instead of Steve to lead a college Bible study—which then grew to 2,000 students overnight. Matt began getting speaking requests from all over West Texas, and Steve began getting really jealous.

After college the phenomenon continued, with Steve working in a rural church where he was never going to get noticed and Matt working in an urban church that exploded with growth. Then something happened that caused the spotlight over Matt's head to go to high beams. Steve writes,

> As if he couldn't rise any faster, Matt was then diagnosed with brain cancer. It soon seemed that everywhere I looked, Matt was there, preaching with a bald scalp and a pronounced cranial scar, testifying to the goodness of God.
>
> While all the truly saved Christians listened with delight, I found myself in the ridiculous position of envying a cancer patient.
>
> He may have had brain cancer, but I was the one who was sick.[5]

God's goodness continued, Matt's life was spared, and his ministry grew even more fruitful. After years of comparison, Steve decided to call Matt one day and confess his envy. Matt said, "That's funny, because there are days when I envy you."

For Steve, this was a watershed moment. He suddenly realized that Matt was simply a servant who, like him, had the potential of looking over at someone else with envy. They were just two brothers on equal footing, leading churches and serving a God who says, "Am I not allowed to do what I choose? Or do you begrudge my generosity?"

God used this moment of raw confession, along with Matt's gracious words, to tear the jealousy from Steve's heart. He is now pleased—not bothered—by the fruit God has produced in Matt's ministry. God has given both of these pastors exactly the gifts, opportunities, and fruit that he wants for them to have. The same, dear sister, is true of me and you.

≈ Is there an individual whose ministry—either in her home, in the church, overseas, or in the community—has been generously rewarded by God? Make a list, and for each situation, record your heart response.

≈ Read Hebrews 13:15. Write out your "sacrifice" by acknowledging God's generosity to the person(s) on your list and praising him for his generosity. Consider whether God wants you to confess your envy, the way Steve did.

≈ Read Exodus 34:14. What is God's name? Why is it good for God to be jealous, but not us? Why does your envy of another person make God jealous?

≈ Read Isaiah 42:5–9. What will God not give away (v. 8)? Who are you jealous of, and how does this compete with God's glory? What one verse or phrase helps lift your focus from your jealous comparison back to God?

For Meditation: Matthew 20:15

> Am I not allowed to do what I choose with what belongs to me? Or do you begrudge my generosity?

When God generously rewards my sister in ministry, I can either stifle God's glory with my jealous protests or multiply his glory with my praise. *God, who am I to begrudge your generosity? I will rejoice in _____'s ministry and life!*

Lesson 4: Lifting Up "Lasts"
Read Matthew 20:1–16

WHEN I SPEAK for moms' groups, I'm always encouraged by how devoted women are to connecting with each other. Yet sometimes, after moving heaven and earth just to make it through the door, moms slip right into the comparison trap.

The differences aren't hard to spot. There's the mom who arrives first, twenty minutes early with her six littles in tow. She smiles sunnily as she drops them off with the childcare workers—each with hair combed and teeth brushed and ready to quote last week's memory verse. She's been up since dawn, has dinner simmering in the slow cooker, and has an extra diaper bag packed and ready in case you forget yours.

Then there's the mom who slips in last, appearing overwhelmed and frazzled. She's twenty minutes late and is wearing her yoga pants from yesterday with a spit-up stain down the right leg. Her new baby is fussing and she is sweating. She has no idea what's for dinner and could really use that extra diaper bag, since she forgot hers and the baby is wet.

If you knew me well, you'd know I am always pushing myself with restarts and goals, trying so hard to be like that first mom, but far more often I am like the last. I run late constantly. I'm frazzled and unprepared. I regularly forget things, hardly ever have a plan for dinner, and am usually wearing yesterday's yoga pants with a stain. Whether you're serving Jesus as a mom or in other ways today, I'd like to call a huddle for the woman who feels like a "last." I'd like to talk to the one who's glancing over at a "first," thinking, *Jesus, have I failed you? I feel like I am seriously lacking here.*

If that's you, I have good news. The parable of the vineyard workers is for us "lasts," too, and offers some sweet encouragement.

Jesus crafted the story as a gentle rebuke for Peter, who was obviously one of the "firsts." But as he told it, Jesus was aware of the other disciples in the circle, too, who were also trying to find themselves in the story (Matt. 19:23, 25).

Remember that Jesus shined two spotlights onto this story. We've listened carefully to the warnings Jesus gave to the "firsts." Now let's listen just as carefully to the encouragement that Jesus gave to the "lasts."

THE MASTER'S CALL

The master hired workers at five different times throughout the day. These later workers didn't select their start group or how many hours they wanted to work. The master did. Notice the question he asked when he went back at 5 p.m. and found them still waiting. "'Why do you stand here idle all day?' They said to him, 'Because no one has hired us'" (Matt. 20:6–7).

Our storyteller wants us to know that these workers weren't lazy. They weren't stubborn or unwilling. They weren't even sitting down. They were standing. Waiting. Hoping to be used by the master. Certainly there are places in the Bible where God corrects our rebellion, laziness, or self-centeredness, but this isn't one of them.

These workers did as much as they could in the time they had. At the end of the day, it was obvious they hadn't accomplished as much, but to their great delight, they received a generous wage. What a kind master!

Now here's the part in the story where we—those who feel like "lasts"—need to lean in and learn something about our own Master and how he sees things. When the 6 a.m. workers grumbled angrily about not getting paid more for more work, the Master didn't let that go. He challenged them. He didn't let the "firsts" get away with acting like they were superior. In his eyes, they *weren't*. If you need proof, just look at the exact same generous payment in every worker's hands!

The master wasn't disparaging the 6 a.m. workers; rather he was *elevating* the 5 p.m. workers. And that's what our God does too. He elevates those who feel small, inferior, or last and reaffirms our worth.

LITTLE IS MUCH

Why would God calculate a servant's worth based on output or raw talent when—in his hands—even the smallest person can become great?

Think of David, the shepherd boy with a slingshot. God used him to bring down Goliath. Think of runaway Moses, who stuttered. God used him to challenge Pharaoh and deliver millions from slavery.

If Jesus could scoop a handful of dust and make a human being out of it, I'm guessing any handful would do. And if he could divide a boy's lunch to feed five thousand, I'm guessing any boy's lunch would do. Jesus is the great multiplier. The amount of talent, wealth, influence, or potential in our measuring cup is of no consequence to Jesus, for he can make up for any lack.

Remember how Paul bragged about his weaknesses instead of his many strengths? He knew that when he was weakest, God was at his most powerful (2 Cor. 12:9). God wants us to learn to see each other and ourselves with new kingdom perspective. If God fills a measuring cup with himself, every small person or small gift or small service has epic potential. The "lasts" hold incredible possibility—not because they are great, but because God is.

BELONGING

When I was a fourth-grade teacher, there were times when one student would treat another as inferior right in front of me. I'm not talking about audacious bullying, just a little shove or a slight taunt. Enough for the "first" to put the "last" in her place. I used these situations strategically by correcting the public behavior publicly and with stern severity.

"Oh no you don't," I would say. "Caroline is a valuable part of this classroom, and you may not *ever* treat her with such disrespect. Do you understand? You need to apologize to her right now."

This did two things for the students looking on. It let the ones who thought of themselves as "firsts" know that I didn't see them as superior. And it let the ones who thought of themselves as "lasts" know that I didn't see them as inferior. They could relax, take risks, and even be silly, knowing that no one would be allowed to mock or belittle them. No, they weren't all alike. But yes, they all belonged and were accepted.

That's how Jesus wants us to see each other. That's why he told the story the way he did, so that the guys grumbling because they weren't treated like "firsts" were challenged. And the ones who knew they were "lasts" were elevated. No matter when we arrived in the kingdom or how much we've accomplished, here's what is true: our master values our work. But our value doesn't come *from* our work. He sees us not as "firsts" or "lasts" but as the ones he called, the ones who belong. To each of us he has said, "You go into the vineyard too" (Matt. 20:7).

Friend, it would be a mistake to add up your kingdom service using the world's measure-up calculator. And it would be a mistake to let others who measure by the lines define the worth of your service. Think forward to the day the sun sets on your vineyard work. You might leave behind twelve Jesus-following children or one teenager whom you mentored. You might have led ten thousand people to Jesus or planted a few seeds. You might have served forty years on the mission field or a handful of days in the church nursery. You just have no idea how God will use even the smallest gift of service you gave.

Something Big

My friend Alicia Bruxvoort dreamed of doing big things for God. She had been using all her free time (which wasn't much as the mom of five young children) to pull together a proposal for a book, which she prayed God would use in spectacular ways.

One day she opened yet another response from a publisher which said the same as the others. "We love your writing. We love your ideas. But because your platform is small, we don't think we could sell enough books." That was the last straw. Alicia shredded the letter and threw it on the floor, then crumpled to a heap where she sat amidst the pieces of paper. With tears streaming, she said, *God, I am done with this dream!* Then she heard him say, *Good.*

What? That's not what she wanted to hear. *I was doing this for you, Lord!* she said. But she sensed him whispering, *I don't think so.*

That night before bed, God arranged for another letter to be delivered to Alicia. It was an email from a young mom named Callie who had attended the moms' group where Alicia spoke that morning.

Callie hadn't planned to be there. Actually, she wasn't even part of the group. But after dropping her daughter off at preschool, Callie was driving by and noticed the church's beautiful steeple. She prayed, "God, I wish I could know that you really do love me." Then she sensed God telling her to pull over and go into the church.

Callie still couldn't believe she'd done it. It seemed crazy, but she pulled into the parking lot and entered the building, which was dark and quiet. She almost turned around, but then she heard voices and followed their sound. She slipped into the back of the room as Alicia was speaking, telling the women just how much Jesus adored them.

Callie sat listening and trying not to cry. She knew that Jesus had sent Alicia to prove his love to her, and now she was writing to tell Alicia that before she left the church, she had given her life back to the one who really loves her.

That morning, Alicia had driven thirty minutes to speak in a musty church basement to twenty moms with fifteen nursing babies on their laps. And she had gone home with a potted plant. It hadn't been glamorous. To Alicia it had seemed like a small and insignificant way to serve—especially compared to the big things she wanted to do for God. Yet God had taken her small act of service and done something *big*.

Friend, do you see yourself as one of the "lasts"? Do you compare and worry that you're not doing enough or that your work for Jesus doesn't measure up? Wherever you place yourself in line, Jesus comes to you and says, *Stop looking down the row. Stop measuring yourself with my other workers. You're here to serve me. So simply pour out what you have, and remember that in my hands anything is possible.*

≈ Tell about a time that you've felt like a "last" compared to other servants of Christ. What difference does it make to know that God challenges anyone who says your work should be valued less?

≈ Read John 6:5–13. What did Jesus ask Philip? Why? Jesus sometimes puts our limitations before us as a test. What small, limited way is Jesus asking you to serve him today? Write a prayer, trusting him to multiply what you will give.

≈ Read 2 Corinthians 12:7–10. What "thorn" keeps you from doing
all that you'd like to do for Jesus? How has your thorn kept you
from being conceited? Write verse 10, inserting your personal
thorn. Pray that this might be true.

For Meditation: 2 Corinthians 12:9

> But he replied, "My kindness is all you need. My power
> is strongest when you are weak." So if Christ keeps giv-
> ing me his power, I will gladly brag about how weak I
> am." (CEV)

In God's hands, even my most insignificant act of service can be multiplied and used greatly. He sees me not as a "first" or "last" but as one
of the workers who belongs. *Lord, help me to stop looking down your row of
servants and comparing. Please display your power in my weaknesses.*

Chapter Six
Comparing Status

IN MY EARLY twenties, I was filling up my car and noticed a friend from high school at the next pump. We greeted each other, then continued to chat while our tanks were filling. Then, driving away, I realized something embarrassing.

In that brief exchange of about a minute and a half, I had slipped in details about my new job, my new car, and my new boyfriend—who also had a really good job and a really nice car. I couldn't remember if I had asked her any questions about herself, and if so, I had no idea what the answers were.

In the time it took to fill my gas tank, I had tried to top off my status with such blatant arrogance that it turned my stomach. I still feel chagrin, decades later. How ugly and unbecoming my self-absorbed me-focus is. How I need Jesus in order to become me-free.

As we look in on the disciples during some of their final interactions with Jesus, their me-focus on status is just as unbecoming. But as we turn our eyes to Jesus, who quietly empties his cup, we find both compelling beauty and guidance for our path ahead.

Lesson 1: Equal Opportunity
Read Mark 9:33–37

HAYLEY HAS ALWAYS struggled with feeling inferior to her younger sister. Mari is driven, successful, and beautiful. She's a medical doctor, married to an attorney. They have four beautiful children, own an impressive house, and drive brand new cars. Hayley loves her life, but she admits it's simpler. She has a quieter personality, and she's content to stay home with her two kids. Hayley and her electrician husband live in a less impressive house, and drive not-new cars.

When Hayley was growing up, her dad would help Mari with her softball pitch or free throws, but Hayley was never into sports. She had nothing to make her stand out, and she wondered, *"Dad, do you see me too?"*

Recently, Hayley overheard her dad telling someone about Mari's new house and new job. When the person asked about Hayley, he said, "Oh, Hayley's fine. She's just home taking care of her kids." She realized then that things are always going to be this way. The status gap between Mari and her will only widen—which will only cause her dad to keep turning Mari's way.

Status is achieved when you outrank someone. You're somehow "better" than they are. It isn't necessarily about having more but about showing that you *are* more. What you have, what you do, or what you've accomplished are just the proof. Status can't be achieved on a desert island—you need other people around, and you need to measure up.

Do you, like Hayley, feel outranked by someone at work, in your family, in your neighborhood, or at church? Does your life seem small next to theirs? Listen carefully, because Jesus has something he'd like you to know about status in the upside-down kingdom.

WHO'S THE GREATEST NOW?

One day, on the road into Capernaum, Jesus's disciples got into a big argument about who was the greatest. It was the equivalent of holding their measuring cups side by side and arguing about whose cup was more full of importance. We aren't told what sparked the argument, but as a Comparison Girl, I have a guess.

Just a page back is the mountaintop story, where Jesus let his humanity fall away and revealed his lightning streak–colored glory (Mark 9:2–10). But not all the disciples had seen it. Only the three who were invited. And while Jesus forbid them from talking about it, this probably didn't prevent them from using raised eyebrows and body language to communicate just how epic the experience had been. The Bible doesn't tie that event to the disciples' argument on the Capernaum road, but it's not hard to imagine how the exclusivity of such an awe-inspiring event might have sparked a "Who's the greatest now?" debate among the twelve men.

At the house, Jesus asked what they had been discussing back on the Capernaum road, but the disciples said nothing. They knew they were wrong. It was obvious they had been focused on the lines, not the spout.

Red-Letter Comparison: "If anyone would be first, he must be last of all and servant of all" (Mark 9:35).

In response to their silence, Jesus sat down to share another red-letter comparison: "If anyone would be first, he must be the last of all and servant of all" (Mark 9:35). Notice that Jesus didn't criticize the disciples for wanting to be great; he just redefined what greatness looks like. In the kingdom, the great ones aren't those who have achieved first place status; they're the ones choosing to be last.

Ours is a world where it's natural to want to place first, be ranked first, or be chosen first. We want the measuring cup that's filled to the top line. Yes, we know there are limited places on the top tier, but that only makes them more desirable. We scramble and push, trying to edge each other out, with the ultimate goal of achieving the status of being first.

But in Jesus's kingdom, things are upside down. We aren't saddled with a tiered status system, where we have to edge others out or differentiate ourselves in a crowd. All of us can pursue greatness all the time by choosing to be last, not first.

Bottom-Tier Medalists

Think of the Olympics, where the gold medalist stands proudly alone on the top tier of the podium, proving her status by distancing herself from the other competitors.

In Jesus's kingdom, it's upside down. The "firsts" are grouped together in a wide space on the bottom tier. These "firsts" are willing to serve anyone, great and small. It's the "lasts" who clamor for the top tier. By trying to distinguish themselves from those who seem small, these "lasts" preclude themselves from being rewarded.

Jesus wanted his disciples to see that kingdom greatness isn't about status. It isn't achieved by being the lonely one at the top. It's about being the one-among-the-many at the all-inclusive bottom. He taught them, "If anyone would be first, he must be last of all and servant of all" (Mark 9:35). Notice the "all"? Last of *all*. Servant of *all*. Greatness in the kingdom is anything but exclusive. To make this point, Jesus used an object lesson involving the smallest person of *all* in the room.

He took a child—probably a baby or toddler from their host family—and placed him in the middle of those twelve men. Did he cry? Considering he was surrounded by twelve strangers, I think yes. So here Jesus created a need, then he opened his arms to that need—literally. He picked up the baby and held him close.

Jesus was saying, "You want to be great? Here's how to do it." Then he picked up a baby. He showed that in the kingdom, the great ones aren't on the top tier, comparing down. They're on the bottom tier, *bending* down and receiving the needs of others into their arms.

Today, if Jesus gathered the most influential pastors and leaders of our day and held a training on greatness, I think he'd do the same thing. "You want to be great?" he'd ask, then he would show them how by leaning down to pick up a baby.

Mom Status

One year when my son played soccer, someone mentioned that another mom from the team was a medical doctor. Immediately my opinion of her shot up. "Oh! I didn't know she was a *doctor*," I replied. I figured she was just a mom, like me.

In all my years of being a mother, nobody—after knowing me for a while—has said, "Oh! I didn't know you were a *mom*." Motherhood doesn't naturally earn me status in the world. But in Jesus's upside-down kingdom—where the great ones lean down and serve—motherhood actually offers vast opportunity.

Jesus wasn't saying that caring for children was the only way to be great. That's not what the disciples went on to do. Yet by picking up a baby to demonstrate greatness, Jesus made it pretty clear that in the kingdom, "greatness" and caring for the small people—whether literal children or those considered "small"—are not mutually exclusive.

Have you picked up a baby today? Have you spent seasons of your life picking up babies? Have you spent decades serving your family, or tending to a family member with special needs or failing health? These might not seem like gold-medal-worthy accomplishments in the world. But in Jesus's heavenly economy, those who serve are the great ones. Spending the day receiving children into your arms for the sake of Christ doesn't cost you status; it makes you a bottom-tier, gold-medal "first."

RECEIVING BABIES

As women, we were designed by God with the unique ability to "receive a child" not just into our arms but into our wombs. This is a beautiful way to serve another human being, but also quite costly. Some would say too costly.

Back when I was tending to smelly diapers and chins dripping with drool, I read an article by philosopher Linda Hirshman, who, in retort to some backlash she received, wrote, "Everybody started hating Linda, apparently, when I published an article . . . saying that women who quit their jobs to stay home with children were making a mistake. Worse, I said that the tasks of housekeeping and child rearing were not worthy of the full time and talents of intelligent and educated human beings."[1] Linda might have been surprised by her hate mail, but I wasn't.

As I pictured Linda looking down with disgust at me as I—a college-educated woman—changed yet another diaper, I took comfort in the fact that Jesus saw my work differently.

Jesus's model of greatness frees women to consider motherhood a viable option for a great life—not merely a potential-quashing obstacle. Jesus says that when we receive children into our arms, our laps, or even our bodies, we receive God (Mark 9:37) and welcome his fellowship and nearness. There's even a sense in which, through pregnancy, this is literally true, since each human baby bears the image of God.

Now, obviously God does not call us all to have children. Anna, Miriam, Deborah, and Martha served God in great ways, yet (presumably) not through motherhood. And God doesn't call us all to have the same number of children either. Sarah and Hannah each had one.

I was once told by an older woman in my church that as a godly wife, I should have as many babies as my body was able to produce—likely between fourteen and eighteen children. Friends, I can tell you that it was not pursuit of status that kept me from having eighteen children; it was pursuit of sanity! We should be careful about spelling out for each other what "serving God" looks like—especially since Jesus often leads us in completely opposite directions. He might invite one of us to serve him by mothering eighteen children and another to serve him in ways completely *other* than mothering. Mothering isn't the only way to pursue greatness in the kingdom, but it *is* one way. That's my point.

Before we move on, allow me to speak softly to the woman who would love to serve the Lord by growing a family but, for whatever reason, cannot. Please, oh please, do not let the enemy use God's Word (of all things) to give rise to your measure-up jealousy through comparison. Dear sister, you have just as many opportunities to achieve greatness in the kingdom of God! Nothing, absolutely *nothing*, is preventing you from a gold-medal life at the wide space at the base of the podium.

Think of Jesus. Yes, he held lots of babies, but he didn't have children of his own. If you wouldn't dare argue that Jesus's life was less great because he had no children, then please don't argue that yours is either. **Jesus's kingdom offers equal opportunity for women in the truest sense.** No woman is excluded from any opportunity, since she can achieve greatness wherever she can serve. This might occur behind a mahogany desk in a corner office of a high-rise building. Or it might take place in the middle of a kitchen filled with sticky messes and whiny children.

Friends, every time we bend down to serve, we pursue kingdom advancement. And every time we open our arms to someone "small," we receive Jesus and welcome God as our companion (Mark 9:37).

≈ Write Mark 9:35, emphasizing the word "all" with large lettering. Draw some large stick people and put the names of several who seem "small" to you. Now draw a small stick person of yourself, and write one way you will serve each one.

≈ Read Mary's song in Luke 1:46–55, after she greeted Elizabeth with the baby Jesus in her womb. What is Mary's response to this pregnancy (vv. 46–49)? Record what Mary says about the upside-down ways of the kingdom (vv. 51–53).

≈ Read Philippians 2:3–4. Make a list of ways to "count others as more significant than yourself" (v. 3). Now title your list "Equal Opportunity for Greatness." Put a star by the services that you want to pursue with the most enthusiasm.

For Meditation: Mark 9:35

> If anyone would be first, he must be last of all and ser-
> vant of all.

In Jesus's kingdom, no woman is excluded from any opportunity, since every woman can achieve greatness wherever she serves. *Lord, help me to be the servant of* all, *to exclude no one, and to invite you near.*

Lesson 2: Making Myself Small
Matthew 18:1–4 and Philippians 2:1–11

MY HUSBAND HAD been working at an international wholesale food distribution company only a few months when we attended the annual Christmas party. I was standing in the atrium while my husband checked our coats when I noticed an older man who was apparently also waiting for someone. I greeted him, and he kindly chatted with me, asking about my husband's position and our holiday plans.

As we talked, I noticed that this man seemed to know *everyone*. As people arrived, he would raise a hand and call greetings, then each time turn his full attention back to me. I also noticed that although people replied cheerily, no one came over to chat. It was as if there was some invisible ring around this kindly gentleman and me. Well into our friendly exchange, I noticed his name tag. I was speaking with John Gordon, one of the owners of the company. More accurately, I was monopolizing John Gordon, and he was treating me with the utmost attention and respect.

Quickly, I excused myself with a reddening face, and joined everyone else who was showing honor by not monopolizing the man putting on the party.

If you asked me to name some families of status in my community, the Gordon family would top the list. John Gordon is one of the wealthiest, most influential and respected businessmen in West Michigan. And somehow his kindness toward little me makes him seem even greater, don't you think? That's what humility does. Rather than diminishing greatness, humility amplifies it. It makes great people greater yet.[2]

GREATEST DISCIPLE AWARD

The disciples had been clinging to the promise of a Messiah for their whole lives. A king would come and set his people free . . . which obviously meant overthrowing Roman oppression. And now that king was here! The prophecies that had once seemed vague were shaping into vivid mental images. Soon the streets would be clear of Roman soldiers looking down on them and making them feel small. Soon Roman taxes would no longer be shrinking their wealth. The disciples could just see their fathers, siblings, wives, and children all gathering as free people, waving palm branches before Jesus as he sat upon his throne. Their hearts swelled every time they thought of it.

But there was one problem. They didn't know exactly how to arrange *themselves* in this mental image. Which one of them had the most status? Who would be assigned the coveted thrones, positioned to Jesus's right and left? They were wondering, and apparently they had wondered aloud—which sparked their argument back on the road to Capernaum.

In Mark's account, which we looked at last time, the disciples stayed quiet when Jesus asked what they had been discussing. But apparently—according to Matthew's account—somebody broke the silence and asked Jesus to settle the argument. "Who is the greatest in the kingdom of heaven?" they asked (Matt. 18:1). They weren't hoping to learn how to *become* great; they wanted to know who presently *was* great. *Who stands out, Lord? Which of us has the highest rank? If you had to pick right now . . .*

I remember the way my little boys used to come when they wanted me to settle their disputes. They would stand before me, elbowing each other, giving little side shoves, and cutting each other off mid-sentence so they could tell their side of the story. They always wanted me to side with one of them, not both. But I just wanted them to love each other. If they kept this rivalry going, they were both going to get hurt.

That's how Jesus felt about his disciples too. As they come asking Jesus to hand out "greatest disciple" awards, not one of them is trying to stoop and be small. They're using sharp elbows to get past each other and claim stake to top-tier greatness. So Jesus confronts them, and he does so with a baby on his lap.

BE GREAT; BE SMALL

Last time, we watched Jesus demonstrate greatness by picking up a baby. But this time, Jesus expands the object lesson by saying the disciples should become *like* the baby he's holding: "Truly, I say to you, unless you turn and *become like children*, you will never enter the kingdom of heaven. Whoever humbles himself *like this child* is the greatest in the kingdom of heaven" (Matt. 18:3–4, emphasis mine).

Did you see that? In a room full of men vying for status, Jesus points to a baby and says, "Be like this little person." Whoever humbles himself or herself like a child is the greatest in the kingdom of heaven.

When my kids were toddlers, I used a baby gate to keep them in the kitchen area. When Ken would get home from work, they would run to that baby gate and reach up to him. They didn't try to get over the gate or find a way through it. They just looked at their daddy on the other side and lifted their arms. As we approach heaven's gate, this is how Jesus says we must come—as children. No egos, no credentials. No pushing ahead to claim the most prestigious throne. Just needy children who lift their arms to the Father, knowing there is nothing else to do.

When I bring my sharp-elbowed rivalries to Jesus, being told to become small is the last thing I want to hear. I'm trying to puff up, not shrink low. I'm trying to be heard, not muffled.

Truth be told, when I'm feeling threatened by some other person trying to steal my throne, what I really want is for Jesus to put his hands on my shoulders and kindly re-inflate my ego, saying, "Shannon, Shannon . . . Look at your gifts! Look how you're special! Think of all your unique contributions. We need you for this team!" But when Jesus responds to his red-faced, jealous disciples, he does nothing of the sort.

As we've noted before, it's not helpful to respond to a me-focused problem with more me-focus. So instead of reminding the disciples that they are each chosen, selected, and have important work to do—which is true and probably what they would prefer to hear—Jesus replies with what they need to hear.

Jesus goes nuclear and says, "Truly, I say to you, unless you turn and become like children, you will never enter the kingdom of heaven" (Matt. 18:3). Umm . . . this is drastic. Jesus is telling his chosen twelve that unless they stop aspiring to be the biggest person in the room and start becoming small, they can forget about rising to kingdom greatness; they won't even be able to get *in*. Is there any consequence more extreme?

This comparison game the disciples are playing has "Satan was here" graffiti all over. Their jealous rivalry and selfish ambition indicate they've been listening to the wisdom from below, not the wisdom from above (James 3:14–15). Jesus wants his friends to know that they are in a high-stakes gamble with eternal consequences. And before we brush off Jesus's warning, we should remember that Judas did exactly that.

Friend, stop a moment and evaluate carefully. Are you living by the wisdom from below? Do you crave status and try to fill your measuring cup to prove not just that you have more but that you *are* more? Some of the most chilling verses of the Bible are warnings for those who consider themselves disciples yet will hear Jesus say, "I never knew you; depart from me" (Matt. 7:23).

We know that people won't be turned away from the kingdom because of what they did or didn't do (Rom. 11:6). Yet Jesus plainly calls out the traits these deceived people have in common. They were the ones who didn't bend down. They didn't serve. They didn't even see those in need (see Matt. 25:31–46). Could it be that they were too busy elbowing past everyone to claim top-tier status? May this never be true, dear sisters, of me or you.

LITTLING

We often talk about "being humbled" as something that happens *to* us. But there's a big difference between being humbled (or even humiliated) against our will and actively choosing to humble ourselves. It's the *choice* to be humble—to live by the spout, not the lines—that God delights in.

Humility is the choice to see ourselves as small. It's a "littling" of self,[3] but to be clear, it's not *be*littling of self. **The humble person does not set aside her own dignity.** She doesn't pretend that her measuring cup is emptier than it actually is. Humbling ourselves doesn't mean we stop doing the things we're good at or start denying that there are gifts and resources filling our cups. That's not how Jesus humbled himself.

Jesus never denied that he was God's Son or that he had authority and power. He didn't disclaim his greatness and worth, but he *did* make himself small. When Jesus exhorted the disciples to humble themselves and become small like the baby in his lap, he could have added, "Like I did."

BECOMING A BABY

I adore babies, but I can't imagine *becoming* one. To not be able to hold my head up? To need diapers and be strolled about? To be spoon-fed mushy carrots? Obviously, in my life's final chapters, none of this will be outlandish. But to choose it? That *does* seem outlandish to me. I can't imagine opting to have someone wipe the drool from my chin or help me into the bath.

Yet this is what Jesus—the greatest being of the entire universe—willingly chose! And he didn't make this become-a-baby choice as a man; he made the choice as *God*.

For Jesus, there is not one Hubble photograph that reveals something unfamiliar. No research study will ever prove something he doesn't already know. No advancement will ever seem groundbreaking to Jesus, because he had it all in mind when he first spoke our universe into existence.

This is the king who chose to leave the glory of heaven, with angel worship echoing through every corridor, to tuck himself into embryo-size smallness. *This* is the king who was toted about on the hip of his teenage mother. *This* is the king who set aside his mental brilliance to learn carpentry from his adoptive father.

Before King Jesus invited anyone into his upside-down kingdom, he lived his upside-down message. He emptied himself of status and made himself small by serving others instead of demanding to be served. Jesus ultimately humbled himself by dying on the cross, the most extravagant act of humility the world has ever known. And precisely because of Jesus's supreme humility, God exalted him to the highest place (Phil. 2:8–9).

Our God loves humility. When Jesus warned the disciples to stop seeking "greatest disciple" status and pursue humility, it was because he wanted them to have God's favor and the multiplying blessings of heaven. When Jesus folded himself into Mary's womb, he emptied himself of status, but not greatness. And his humility only magnified his greatness even more. This can be true for you and me—the disciples of Jesus—as well. I become greater and more honorable only as I learn to become the smallest person in the room.

≈ Write or print Philippians 2:5-10. Draw a downward arrow above any words that indicate humility or "littling" of self, and an upward arrow above any words that talk about expanding or magnifying.

≈ Picture yourself in various "rooms"—at home, work, church, and other social situations. Draw boxes in your journal representing each, and ask God to reveal specific ways he would like you to become the smallest person in the room. Record your commitments inside each "room."

≈ As "sheep" we will follow Jesus's example by humbling ourselves and serving others. Read Matthew 25:31-46 and make a list of the five things the sheep did, listed in verses 35-36. Have you done any of these things? How might these activities be evidences of your humility? How is God inviting you to respond?

For Meditation: Matthew 18:4

> Whoever humbles himself like this child is the greatest
> in the kingdom of heaven.

Humility doesn't mean I pretend my measuring cup is empty or set aside my dignity. Humility is emptying myself of status and becoming the smallest person in the room. *Lord, help me to become more great as I practice "littling" myself in humility.*

Lesson 3: Seating Requests
Read Matthew 20:20–28

IN 2006, THE Barrick family was hit head-on by a drunk driver going eighty miles an hour. Their daughter, fifteen-year-old Jen, was not expected to live, but after a series of miracles, she survived. Jen now lives with a brain injury that has altered her life forever—but in the best way. Before the accident, Jen had prayed privately that Jesus would help her become bold. Today, she speaks of him with unbridled delight before thousands, telling of the miracles God has done.[4] I've been in the audience and heard her pray, "With you, Daddy, we know the best is yet to come!"

I had the privilege of meeting Jen and her mom, Linda, at a conference this year. In her sweet way, Linda said to a little group of us, "Why don't we find a place to pray together?" So behind a curtain, we got on our knees and lifted our requests to God. There in that circle, I told the Lord that I want what Jen has—her passionate joy and absolute trust. Yet I confessed I don't want the suffering that has delivered Jen to such a pure, heaven-minded focus.

At one point, I prayed, "Lord, I surrender to you all that I hold dear. Even my children . . ." My voice cracked as I thought of all the Barrick family has endured, and my words trailed off, but Linda continued with strength and joy, praying, "But Lord, we know that you have not given us a spirit of fear. We have nothing to fear when you are with us!"

It was such a precious reminder from a mama who has laid down many dreams for her family and endured what none of us would ever choose, but has come through the fire with a heart filled with wonder and joy.

A MOM ON HER KNEES

There was another mom who dropped to her knees before Jesus one day on the road to Jerusalem. It was Salome, the mother of James and John, and she had come to present a request.

Salome clearly loved the Lord and was proud of her sons for following him. And her firm conviction that Jesus would one day sit on David's throne demonstrated beautiful faith. But I'm afraid Salome's intentions, as she got onto her knees, were not to make herself small before Jesus. She had just the opposite in mind.

"Say that these two sons of mine are to sit, one at your right hand and one at your left, in your kingdom," she said to Jesus (Matt. 20:21). Salome wanted her sons to be recognized, to have importance and influence and access to Jesus. She wanted them to achieve greatness, but she misunderstood what greatness *was*. Like her sons, she thought greatness involved being greater *than* the others. Just like Comparison Girls of today, Salome's perspective was skewed by the measure-up world that we're all part of. And what's more, she was using "auntie leverage" to gain status.

If you compare notes on the three women who were at the foot of Jesus's cross, you'll see that Salome is the sister of Mary, Jesus's mother (John 19:25). Which means that she is Aunt Salome to Jesus and that James and John are his cousins.[5] So this isn't just a random woman kneeling to make a request. This is a woman who is trying to use her "in" to make a seating request for her sons.

And here is how Jesus responds to Aunt Salome. He says, "You do not know what you are asking" (Matt. 20:22). It's because she was picturing thrones and honor, not crosses and prison cells for her precious boys.

Those of us who are moms have such longings for our children. We see their gifts and potential like nobody else does, and we dream of the ways God might use them for his glory. Yet as we plead with God to make our children great, like Salome, our own desires for greatness get braided in. This goes for our grandkids, mentees, and friends as well. We attach our success to their status.

When we kneel on behalf of ourselves or others, bringing to Jesus our requests for kingdom greatness, we're a bit like Salome. We don't know what we're really asking. Because in the kingdom, when God calls a person to extraordinary greatness, he first empties her measuring cup in extraordinary ways.

THE WAY UP IS DOWN

Jesus turned from Salome with a question for James and John. "Are you able to drink this cup that I am to drink?" he asked. They said, "We are able" (Matt. 20:22). But since they didn't know what they had asked, they also didn't know what they'd answered.[6]

Jesus, who had wrapped himself in human limitations, told them he couldn't be sure of the seating arrangements in heaven. But he did know one thing: his suffering would precede his glory. Which is the very thing he had just been talking about.

On the road to Jerusalem, he had pulled his disciples to the side for an object lesson, saying, "See, we are going up to Jerusalem" (Matt. 20:18). But Jesus wanted his disciples to see that in the kingdom, the way down is up. Once they arrived in Jerusalem, he would be mocked, flogged, and crucified. Then on the third day, he'd rise again.

Jesus used stark, frank language. He was teaching them the upside-down ways of the kingdom and using himself as the example. Yes, Jesus would be raised from the dead, but not before he was lowered into the grave. Yes, he would ascend to the highest throne, but not before he was devastatingly humbled on the cross (Phil. 2:8–9). In the kingdom, the way up is always down. Did they see?

Enter Salome with some of the most cringeworthy timing ever. Somehow she thought this was the right moment to ask, "Can my boys be picked for those two most prestigious thrones?"

Oh, Salome, how I relate to you. I also have heard the story of the cross and tell Jesus I'm ready to follow. And I also get on my knees and beg him to make my children great for the kingdom. Perhaps God *will* choose one of my kids for standout purposes, but if that is true, it will be accompanied with a cup of bitter suffering to drink down. When I come to Jesus with eyes sparkling, saying, "Can my kid be picked for kingdom greatness?" it's clear that, like Salome, I don't know what I'm asking.

A CUP OF SUFFERING

Nobody longs for suffering. Nobody thirsts for the cup that Jesus is about to drink. James and John certainly didn't. And even Jesus, on the night he was betrayed, prayed, "My Father, if it be possible, let this cup pass from me; nevertheless, not as I will, but as you will" (Matt. 26:39).

Red-Letter Comparison: "Whoever would be first among you must be your slave, even as the Son of Man came not to be served but to serve" (Matt. 20:27–28).

On the side of that Jerusalem road with Aunt Salome on her knees and his cousins bravely vowing to follow him to the bitter end, only Jesus could see what was up ahead. Did James and John truly want the positions at his right and left? Because those spots would be occupied by two men hanging on two crosses. Jesus's cross would come before his throne. His bitter cup before glory. Once again, to help them understand the kingdom, Jesus gave another red-letter comparison: "Whoever would be first among you must be your *slave*, even as the Son of Man came not to be served but to *serve*, and to *give* his life as a ransom for many" (Matt. 20:27–28, emphasis added).

Jesus, their leader, had come to serve. He was about to take a path with a sharp downward slope. In a short time, he would be a slave in chains with a cross on his back. Will James and John follow? Will they drink from Jesus's cup of suffering? Will they loyally give their lives?

As the next chapters of their lives reveal, the answer is no, then yes. The night of Jesus's arrest, the disciples, including James and John, weren't even devoted enough to stay awake and pray (Matt. 26:40). But then, by the power of the Spirit, both brothers put Jesus's great worth on display by laying down their lives for his sake.

SINGLED OUT FOR GREATNESS

Some fourteen years later,[7] when Salome got the shocking news of her son James's death—cut short by Herod's sword—I wonder if she reflected back to that day on the road to Jerusalem. I wonder if she remembered how she had dropped to her knees and, with sparkling eyes, asked Jesus to take her seating request. It couldn't have been easy to hear about the perverse delight of the Jewish leaders in response to Herod's brutality toward her son (Acts 12:2–3). Did Salome drink Jesus's cup of suffering with the same faith that she first approached him?

And did she return to her knees the day her John was taken in chains to Patmos because of his testimony about Jesus (Rev. 1:9)? She had raised her boys to be strong men of principle, and she must have had inner strength herself. Did she remain true to her own conviction that Jesus would one day take his place on the throne? John was an old man by the time he wrote Revelation, telling of his privileged glimpse into heaven and Jesus's throne (see Rev. 21), so it's doubtful that Salome had the delight of reading it. But if she did somehow have the privilege of reading her boy's words, which have brought such brightness and hope to the people of God, imagine her tears of joy and honor!

When Salome kneeled before Jesus asking him to make her boys great, she had no earthly idea what she was asking or what would be asked of her. And we don't know either. We may dream of being singled out for kingdom greatness, but none of us thirst for the cup of suffering that precedes it. So here is what we must determine. Will we surrender to God's purposes for both ourselves and the people we love? Will we willingly take our measuring cups and pour everything out?

Here was Salome's reality. She suffered greatly and would be rewarded (Mark 10:29–30). Her sons also suffered, but one day she would see them sitting on heaven's thrones (Matt. 5:11–12; 19:28). Salome's suffering was temporary, and it can't compare to the glory she'll experience when Jesus establishes his kingdom (Rom. 8:18). The same, dear sister, is true for you.

≈ Has God asked you to humble yourself in extravagant ways? How has he used this for his glory?

≈ Read Romans 8:18, 26–30. Choose a phrase that brings you comfort and write it in your journal several times.

≈ Read Revelation 21:1–14, keeping in mind that this was written by John. What perspective does this give to your current hopes and sorrows? What significance do you think verse 12 had for John?

≈ Get on your knees before the Lord, and surrender your ideals of greatness—for yourself, your children, or others—to him. Say as Jesus did, "Not my will but yours be done."

For Meditation: Romans 8:18

> The sufferings of this present time are not worth comparing with the glory that is to be revealed to us.

Extraordinary kingdom greatness will involve emptying my measuring cup in extraordinary ways. *Lord, I want to surrender my ideals of greatness for myself and others. Help me to drink the cup of suffering you set before me, knowing that with you, there is nothing to fear.*

Lesson 4: Mending Circles
Read Matthew 20:20–28

IN SOME PLACES, "leader" and "superior" are interchangeable terms. But the church isn't one of those places.

In the body of Christ, if Jesus gives you the gift of leadership, it's no different than the other gifts. Leading is just another way to tip your measuring cup and serve. James and John, however, didn't always see it this way. To them, leadership was a prop. A seat to sit on. A way to elevate themselves above the rest and find status.

SEATS OF HONOR

Peter, James, and John were part of Jesus's inner circle. Of the three, we hear about Peter the most.

He was the one to cast his net on the other side of the boat, walk on water, and pull the coins from the fish's mouth. Peter also had a bad habit of saying the wrong thing. The time Jesus was transfigured on the mountaintop, Peter was the one to suggest building three booths—which prompted God to cut in from heaven and tell Peter to be quiet and listen to Jesus (Matt. 17:1-7). Another time, when Peter pulled Jesus aside to confront him, Jesus said, "Get behind me, Satan!" (Matt. 16:23). Being called "Satan" by Jesus? Not good.

You don't quickly recover from grandiose mistakes like these, so back when Jesus mentioned twelve thrones surrounding Jesus's glorious one (Matt. 19:28), James and John must have come to the lightning-fast conclusion that Peter wouldn't be a candidate for two best seats. Which left *them*. It was obvious. But to eliminate any surprises, they sent their mom in to seal the deal.

And what did the other disciples think about this? "And when the ten heard it, they were indignant at the two brothers" (Matt. 20:24). I'm guessing Peter's indignance was the loudest. *Who do you guys think you are? Where do you expect me to sit . . . at your feet?*

By trying to claim these two seats of honor, James and John are sending the inherent, condescending message: "We think we're more important than you guys." That's how status works. You can't scramble to the highest throne without pushing others down. You can't elbow your way to the center without pushing others to the outside.

It's clear these two are clamoring for status. What about the other dagger-shooting ten? While we understand how they felt, isn't their outrage also fueled by desire for status? Their indignation and disgust are also sending a message: "We would *never* stoop as low as you guys have."

The twelve disciples were at risk of a ten-two split, which is exactly what happened to the twelve tribes of Israel. And for the same reasons.

Two Sets of Advice

Hundreds of years prior—back when Israel was still operating as a free, twelve-tribe nation—there was a new king being instated named Rehoboam. The people, who were tired of being treated like slaves, were asking about his leadership style. So Rehoboam got advice from two sources on how to respond.

The older advisers wisely said, "If you will be a servant to this people today and serve them, and speak good words to them when you answer them, then they will be your servants forever" (1 Kings 12:7). Leaders who humbly serve their people inspire their people to also serve.

Rehoboam, however, went with the advice of his peers, who told him to crack the whip and lift himself up by pushing the people down to their knees. "You thought my father was bad?" Rehoboam asked the people. "My father disciplined you with whips, but I will discipline you with scorpions" (1 Kings 12:14). His arrogance and condescension ultimately caused Israel's ten-two tribe split. Which means the disciples are about to repeat history.

A Leader in Red

I once heard about an executive director at a corporation who told her team that she would be wearing a red dress to the Christmas party, so they were not allowed to wear red. She wanted to stand out and be set apart—which of course only made them all want to show up in red.

Someone who is condescending—who belittles, patronizes, or demeans—is always trying to stand apart, no matter what color she's wearing. She wants you to know that she is on the top tier and you are not. She wants to send the message that she's superior.

Jesus has been trying to train his disciples to have exactly the opposite goal of the director in red. Instead of clamoring to the top so that they can look down, Jesus's followers are to *serve*. And the leaders simply go first. Remember the smorgasbord style of spiritual gift sharing we talked about in chapter one? As everyone begins to tip their measuring cups simultaneously and serve one another, a unique sort of circle forms. Insecurities melt and tiers level out. As members share and receive, they all give each other a place to belong.

Launch Training

This is exactly what was *not* happening among the twelve disciples. After what James and John just pulled, nobody was giving *anybody* else a place to belong.

The irony is striking. Here are the twelve men Jesus hand selected to form the launch team for his unity-characterized church. Yet after three years of training for the upside-down kingdom, they're all ready to throw punches in a measure-up fight—and this on the way to Jerusalem, where Jesus will be crucified.

So what does Jesus do? He calls an impromptu discipleship huddle there on the Jerusalem road (Matt. 20:25). No doubt, as the men grouped up, the ten-two split was visually obvious—each group on its side of the line, seething with nostril-flaring arrogance.

I half expect Jesus to say, "You *twelve*. I say one word about thrones, and you're in a brawl about who sits where." But Jesus is amazingly gentle. He doesn't call anyone out. He doesn't bark orders about how things have got to change around here. Instead, the Master of teachable moments capitalizes on this opportunity to disciple. Jesus models kingdom leadership that draws everyone in, rather than pushing anyone out.

"You know that the rulers of the Gentiles lord it over them, and their great ones exercise authority over them," Jesus begins (Matt. 20:25). Yes, they knew all about the Roman leadership style. Their Roman-occupied cities were filled with soldiers, guards, swords, and crosses. Rome was all about rising to power by crushing those beneath them. The Jews despised their Roman captors. "It shall not be so among you," said Jesus. (Matt. 20:26)

Jesus was using a negative example to show the disciples who they're not. It's like the wise advice you might offer to a group of employees or students or athletes whose leader is a self-centered tyrant: "You see how demeaning and patronizing she is, right? See how she's only out for herself? Don't treat each other the way she treats you." Jesus was holding up the arrogant, domineering, status-seeking leadership style of Rome as a point of contrast and saying, "It shall not be so among you" (Matt. 20:26). I picture him leaning forward and emphasizing every word.

It. Shall. Not. Be. So.

This was both a comfort and a warning. The ten didn't have to worry about the two getting away with a throne-claiming power play. But if any of them wanted to achieve kingdom greatness, they'd have to start learning Jesus's red-letter comparisons.

THE GREATNESS OF A SERVANT

"Whoever would be great among you must be your servant, and whoever would be first among you must be your slave" (Matt. 20:26–27).

Notice that Jesus doesn't tell them to stop trying to be great; he just redefines it. The great one is she who serves. This has been Jesus's own leadership style, as he points out: "Even as the Son of Man came not to be served but to serve" (v. 28). And notice that in this moment, he is demonstrating the heart of a servant by drawing each one back to the circle.

In Jesus's kingdom, the great ones don't look down on people; they look into others' eyes and take notice. Some are in high positions and others in low positions, but they all step into their roles as servants. Those who have importance don't realize that it's so because they're too absorbed with taking care of others. They're not shoving people aside or pushing people down. They're leaning in. They're listening. They're caring enough to try to understand.

And what is the result? It's like the advice the older, wiser advisers gave Rehoboam. **People who humbly serve invite others to do the same.**

Of course, in a circle where two are claiming status and the other ten are reacting with disgust, leaning in to serve feels neither normal nor natural. What Jesus was asking of his disciples was both counterintuitive and culturally radical. To serve is to become great. But nobody ever claimed it would be easy.

Yet Jesus wants us each to know that when one servant-hearted disciple puts others first and herself last, it makes a huge difference. She doesn't have to be an official leader. She can be anyone. Greatness is open to all in the kingdom. When that one breaks the trend with me-free humility, the group feels it. It's disarming. Divisions melt and the circle begins to form.

SERVING HER CIRCLE

For twenty years, Brittney had looked forward to her monthly coffee dates with the same group of Christian friends. But this month as she drove to the familiar place, she felt sick to her stomach.

Could she even endure two hours of going around the circle to hear everyone's glowing updates? Could she smile and nod at the reports of Justin making the winning shot, Lizzie getting a scholarship, Jan's vacation in Europe, and Janelle's surprise from her husband—a new car? Brittney turned down a side street in the opposite direction. She just needed a little more time to settle herself before going inside. She still hadn't told any of them that she and Jim were separated.

Twenty-five years. That's how long she'd been trying to be the perfect wife. Then Jim moved out, giving her no explanation. For months now, Brittney has been trying to find her way through this fog. During the past two coffee dates, she hid behind her measure-up facade, pretending all was well. But she left both times feeling so depleted and full of sorrow. *You're a failure, Brittney. Compared with them, you do not measure up.*

"Should I even go in, Lord?" Brittney asked as she drove. The most natural thing would be to withdraw, pull back. Keep driving the opposite direction. But she sensed God saying, *You need people, Brittney. Isolation is not my plan for you.* So, she turned back toward the coffee shop and walked in.

Later that afternoon, as Brittney reflected on another morning of trying to hold herself together in the coffee shop, she decided to do something counterintuitive. Her counselor had been encouraging her to fight her perfectionism—which is really another form of pursuing status—by exposing the underbelly of her flaws. *Here goes . . .* she thought and picked up the phone. It was time to let her friends know what was *really* going on in her life.

As Brittney called her friends one by one and vulnerably shared her heart, she was surprised to hear many of them say, "Brittney, you are not alone. I have struggles that I haven't shared with the group either." Their tender affirmation was such a gift.

The experience awakened a desire for sharing more than "highlight reel" updates with their group. Brittney wasn't the official leader, but she didn't need an official title to be an influence. So she decided to take a brave step and try something new. She invited her coffee friends to a Bible study in her home and was delighted when every single one accepted. As they studied together and shared conviction over sin, vulnerability drew their circle tighter, and they enjoyed even sweeter fellowship.

Me-focused comparison had brought Brittney such sorrow. She had come close to breaking ties with her circle; now she was being healed by it. Leaning in to serve her group instead of pulling away had been counterintuitive and had required me-free humility, but Brittney was amazed at the circle-forming joy it had produced.

Think of your own circle. Is anybody trying to lift herself up or prove she's on the top tier? Is anybody else reacting in self-protectiveness or shooting daggers of disgust? You don't have to be the group leader to influence others. You can help mend the broken parts of your circle by bravely choosing to serve.

≈ In your circle, is anyone claiming status like the "two"—always trying to lift themselves above the others? How do they use condescending attitudes to prove they're on the top tier? Is anyone responding with disgust like the "ten"—reacting in self-protectiveness? How do they communicate disgust or try to reclaim lost status? Which side of the circle are you on? Which side of the circle do you tend to sit on? Make a list of ways you could disarm conflict by serving with humble vulnerability.

≈ Write James 3:17. Which part of this verse will you claim as your circle-mending goal?

≈ Read 1 Kings 12:1–14 and make two lists describing the counsel of the old and the young. Now, for each list, name the people in your life who give you similar counsel. Which list has Jesus's voice? Which people should you be listening to?

≈ Read James 3:12–18. How are the two types of counsel described in 1 Kings 12 similar to the wisdom from above and below? Add the descriptions from James 3 to the two lists you made in the previous exercise. Which type of counsel/wisdom were James and John following in Matthew 20:20–28? How about the other ten? Which counsel/wisdom was Jesus offering?

For Meditation: Matthew 20:25–26

"You know that the rulers of the Gentiles lord it over them. . . . It shall not be so among you."

How am I communicating arrogant superiority or condescending disgust? This causes division in my circle. *Lord, help me be one of the great ones who serves. I want to help form or mend my circle by leaning in, listening, and trying to understand.*

Lesson 5: A Broken and Poured-Out King
Read Luke 22:14–27

THE DAY THAT his younger brother was born, our three-year-old Cole wore a look of bewildered hurt as he wandered around the hospital room. Why was everyone staring at this baby and forgetting to notice him?

We have a video of Cole picking up the tiny newborn hat provided by the hospital and attempting to put it over his own enormous head. Perhaps he thought that wearing the little hat would help garner some of the attention he had lost. He pulled and pulled, but the hat wouldn't stretch over even half of his head. He tugged and yanked, but the thing just popped back off.

"Oh, come *on!*" he kept calling out with rising anger and frustration after each failed attempt. Eventually he flung the hat aside and sulked as the adults stifled laughter. It was cute back then, but if I've learned anything about raising two boys, it's this: jealous rivalry does not stay cute for long.

BIG-HEADEDNESS

The disciples are not cute as they try to stretch the small, servant-minded ways of the kingdom over their big-headedness. They keep hearing Jesus talk about suffering, death, and the cross, but they are like three-year-olds who can't comprehend. The cross just does not *fit* into their grandiose plans for status. So at the most inopportune times, after Jesus has just reminded them that he's on his way to die, the disciples snap back to their same old bickering about who will be the greatest—and they do so repeatedly. It's face-palm worthy.

Read about three of these instances in the following passages, and as you read, mark any words that denote suffering, betrayal, or death with an arrow pointing down (↓). Mark anything about greatness or status with an arrow pointing up (↑).

He was teaching his disciples, saying to them, "The Son of Man is going to be delivered into the hands of men, and they will kill him. And when he is killed, after three days he will rise." But they did not understand the saying, and were afraid to ask him. And they came to Capernaum. And when he was in the house he asked them, "What were you discussing on the way?" But they kept silent, for on the way they had argued with one another about who was the greatest. (Mark 9:31–34)

"The Son of Man will be delivered over to the chief priests and scribes, and they will condemn him to death and deliver him over to the Gentiles to be mocked and flogged and crucified, and he will be raised on the third day." Then the mother of the sons of Zebedee came up to him with her sons, and kneeling before him . . . she said to him, "Say that these two sons of mine are to sit, one at your right hand and one at your left in your

kingdom." (Matt. 20:18–21)

"But behold, the hand of him who betrays me is with

me on the table. . . ." And they began to question one

another, which of them it could be who was going to

do this. A dispute also arose among them, as to which

of them was to be regarded as the greatest. (Luke

22:21–24)

I'm not sure whether Mark, Matthew, and Luke want us to laugh or cry. These are Jesus's closest followers. He is telling them that the road before them goes down before it goes up. He will be humiliated before he's exalted. He will be put in a grave before he's raised. But they just can't conceive of anything remotely downward.

Sadly, during their last moments with Jesus, they're back at it. Rather than treasuring the time with him, the same old fight breaks out about who's the greatest.

A New Passover

By God's providence, Jesus's last meal with his disciples falls exactly on Passover.[8] Historically, Passover commemorated the angel of death *passing over* the Hebrew homes in Egypt that bore lamb's blood on their doorposts, the night before God delivered his people from slavery. But as Jesus ate the Passover with his disciples, he was instituting a new meal of remembrance. From now on, believers would gather to remember *this* night—the night before Jesus, the sacrificial lamb of God, would die to deliver us from our slavery to sin.

The disciples didn't recognize the full significance until afterward, but Jesus knew exactly what he was saying as—during the meal—he chose two objects to represent himself. First, he took a loaf of bread and tore it into pieces. This represented his body, which was about to be broken for them. Then he took a cup of wine, which, poured out, represented his soon-to-be-shed blood. If you're a seasoned believer, don't let familiarity steal the impact of those images from you.

Jesus asked us to remember him as a torn piece of bread and an emptied cup. He was our sacrificial Lamb, torn for his people. He was our King who poured his life out to save us. Jesus continually reminded his disciples—and us—that this was the reason he had come. "For even the Son of Man came not to be served but to serve, and to give his life as a ransom for many" (Mark 10:45). Jesus came to pay our sin debt and free us from this measure-up world.

Surely the disciples ate the bread and drank the cup with grave somberness. Yet their understanding was still pretty skewed. Even after three years of Jesus repeating his red-letter comparisons, they were still fixated on the image of a conquering kingdom—which will come, but much later on the timeline than they realized. When Jesus spoke of suffering and cost, they were picturing valiant sword fights resulting in crowns, thrones, and honor. Not blood dripping down a cross or oozing from a crown of thorns as people sneered.

To be clear, Jesus did anticipate his own exaltation. Hebrews 12:2 says, "For the joy that was set before him [Jesus] endured the cross, despising the shame, and is seated at the right hand of the throne of God." And it's true that Jesus had motivated the disciples with images of crowns and thrones (see Luke 22:29–30). But he had unwaveringly taught that in the upside-down kingdom, being broken and poured out is the precursor to greatness; me-focus and self-promotion are the barriers that hold you back.

So at their last meal with Jesus, the disciples are still focusing on the measure-up lines, not the empty-yourself spout. And ironically, it was Jesus's mention of the most me-focused man in the room that once again sparked another round of, "Who's the greatest now?" It seems so ludicrous! Yet so very possible. So very much like us.

I Would Never

Look at the stark contrast between Jesus and Judas as they sat there at the dinner table. In extreme selflessness, Jesus was preparing to lay His life down for His friends. In evil selfishness, Judas was preparing to make some cash by leading Jesus into a death trap.

When Jesus said, "Behold, the hand of him who betrays me is with me on the table" (Luke 22:21), the disciples immediately turned to each other with questions of who would do such a thing. For once their outrage was entirely appropriate, since Jesus's murder was the greatest atrocity ever committed. But once again their focus slipped from vindicating God to vindicating themselves.

What began with troubled disciples saying, "Is it I, Lord?" quickly shifted to, "I think it's him!" Fingers pointed. Voices raised. Insulted disciples proclaimed with disgust, "I would never!" Then in an equally outrageous shift, "I would never!" morphed into, "Remember, I'm the guy who . . ." And once again they were back to their same old argument: "A dispute also rose among them, as to which of them was to be regarded as the greatest" (Luke 22:24).

When we're accused, we always want to lift ourselves up. When we feel threatened, we resort to ego-gratification. In defensiveness, we push back our chairs and storm off, saying, "I would never!" But self-defense, self-protection, and self-promotion are not the ways of the kingdom. And Jesus's time with his new kingdom officers was drawing to a close.

The One Who Serves

As I watch this scene unfold, I want Jesus to start barking out orders. I want him to call, "Ten-hut!" and point his finger in these guys' faces! Yet in striking patience and long-suffering kindness, Jesus uses these last moments not to rebuke but to teach.

Gently, he draws his self-righteous, infuriated, incensed disciples back to the way of the kingdom: "The kings of the Gentiles exercise lordship over them, and those in authority over them are called benefactors. But not so with you. Rather, let the greatest among you become as the youngest, and the leader as one who serves. For who is the greater, one who reclines at table or one who serves? Is it not the one who reclines at table? But I am among you as the one who serves" (Luke 22:25–27).

Jesus, whose measuring cup is filled with more greatness than could be contained in all the oceans, wanted us to remember him as the one who serves. He was the leader who got on his knees to wash their feet. He is the Lamb whose blood will be spilled for his people. He is the King who will always be called to mind by a torn piece of bread and an empty cup.

And if they are his disciples, they must follow his lead.

A Broken Follower

As a Christian woman living in a democracy, I enjoy vast privileges and protection that women throughout the ages have not. And though I am deeply grateful for my freedom and opportunities, in some ways I think it's harder to live as a "broken and poured out" Christian in "the land of the free."

The world screams for me to stand up for myself, defend my rights, and strive for success. The American dream is all about the lines, not the spout. And the idea of pouring out what others have fought for me to have seems almost disgraceful.

When upside-down themes of heaven—such as submission, laying down rights, brokenness, sacrifice, and repentance—are proclaimed, the people around me do not applaud. Instead, women gather to march against such ideas. They grip their measuring cups, along with their posters and megaphones, tightly between their fists.

But as women who follow Jesus, we must take a narrower path. We must ignore the crowd's roar and listen to our Jesus, who says, "I am the one among you who serves. Follow me."

≈ Read Luke 22:14–20. Either with a group or by yourself, take some time to rehearse what the bread and cup symbolize and to remember Jesus.

≈ How is Jesus inviting you to walk upstream against the world's marching and megaphones and follow him by being "broken and poured out"?

≈ Read Philippians 2:2–4. How do these instructions stand in contrast with the disciples' measure-up behavior at the Last Supper?

≈ Read Philippians 2:5–8. How have these verses, and especially the part about Jesus "emptying himself" in verse 7, gained new significance as you've worked through this book?

For Meditation: Luke 22:19

> And he took the bread. . . . He broke it and gave it to them, saying, "This is my body, which is given for you. Do this in remembrance of me."

Jesus gave me two images to remember him by: a torn piece of bread and an emptied cup. *Lord, help me to pursue brokenness, not perfection. Help me to empty myself of status and serve others as you did.*

Conclusion: "Lord, What About Her?"

ONE NIGHT AFTER Jesus had risen, seven of the disciples went fishing. In the early morning, as they approached the shore, they saw a man who was cooking bread and fish over a charcoal fire.

It was Jesus.

Peter flung himself into the sea to get to shore first, then the others caught up for a grand reunion. They enjoyed breakfast together, then Jesus took a walk with Peter. It was an important conversation. They still hadn't spoken of that moment when their eyes had locked just as the rooster crowed, just after Peter had denied his Lord (Luke 22:61).

Peter knew he had failed miserably. His me-focus in that moment disgusted him, yet amazingly Jesus saw no less potential in Peter. The one who can turn water to wine, multiplies a lunch to feed thousands, and turns weakness to strength is not encumbered by our failings. In fact, Peter's fresh awareness of his weakness would serve him well in the days to come. For when we sense our own emptiness, that's when we invite Jesus to make up for our lack.

"Do you love me, Peter?" Jesus asked three times, giving Peter the opportunity to reverse his betrayals. Each time, Jesus told Peter how to demonstrate his love: by feeding Jesus's sheep. Peter was to tend the flock of followers, now gathering one by one, as they heard of Jesus's resurrection and believed. Peter had an important role to play. Not a measure-up role, but an assignment of pouring himself out for the sake of others.

WHAT'S THAT TO YOU?

Jesus had another bit of input for Peter about what was ahead. There would be a new test, and this time Peter wouldn't cave in to fear and self-protectiveness. In old age Peter—with arms stretched wide on a cross of his own—would bring glory to God in his death (John 21:18–19).

After delivering this somber news, Jesus gave Peter a two-word, all-encompassing instruction: "Follow me" (v. 19). He was to follow in Jesus's footsteps and empty out his life completely.

Peter, craning his neck to see John trailing behind, asked, "Lord, what about this man?" (v. 21). Would John die on a cross too? Would John also be called to sacrifice it all? Peter wanted to know. But Jesus said, "What is that to you? You follow me!" (v. 22).

Comparison Girl, it's time to be done with looking at other people's measuring cups. It's time to stop caving in to our enemy's temptation to compare up in envy or down in disgust. Our Lord has shown such patience with our craning necks and sharp elbows, but now he says it's time to stop. We have too much work involving the spout to be distracted by the measure-up lines.

The measuring cup of the sister beside me might be tipped at a sharper angle or filled with a more exceptional gift. She might be led on a path that dips lower or one that raises her higher. But when I glance sideways and ask, "Lord, what about her?" his answer is, "What is that to you?"

Jesus gives me the same God-glorifying, two-word instruction that he gave Peter and gives to you. To each of us, he says, "Follow me."

LIVING ME-FREE

In this book, we've had the privilege of listening to King Jesus respond directly to people who were comparing in all the same ways we do, deceived by the same evil ruler who comes to steal, kill, and destroy. We've seen our Lord swing wide the narrow gate to his kingdom, offering an escape from our measure-up fear and get-ahead pride. He has made a way for exhausted Comparison Girls like us to stop our endless striving to fill our measuring cups on our own and be filled by his Spirit instead.

As we fall in step with Jesus, pouring out who we are and what we have, the lines on the sides of our measuring cups become irrelevant. As we bend down to serve each other, we stop worrying about measuring up. As we collectively tip our cups forward, we give each other a place to belong.

This life is what I've been waiting for. It's who I want to be. And it's what I want for you, too, my fellow Comparison Girl. For living by the spout, not the lines, is the way Jesus reinstates our freedom, confidence, and joy.

So are you ready? Let's leave me-first comparison behind. Let's follow our Jesus and inherit eternal life together. Let's discover a me-free life that is truly beyond compare.

> For this light momentary affliction is preparing for us an eternal weight of glory *beyond all comparison*, as we look not to the things that are seen but to the things that are unseen. For the things that are seen are transient, but the things that are unseen are eternal. (2 Cor. 4:17–18, emphasis added)

Notes

Chapter One: From Measuring Up to Pouring Out

1. Meghan Holohan, "6 Infamous Arsonists and How They Got Caught," Mental Floss, January 3, 2012, http://mentalfloss.com/article/29633/6-infamous-arsonists-and-how-they-got-caught. See also Matthew Rosenbaum, "Inside the Mind of an Arsonist," ABC News, January 2, 2012, https://abcnews.go.com/US/mind-arsonist-head-los-angeles-fire-starters/story?id=15274504.

2. See Jude 1:6 and Revelation 12:9. Also, note that in Isaiah 14:12–14, Isaiah is speaking of the king of Babylon, yet he attributes this king's rebellion to Satan's work in the background.

3. I appreciate *The Voice* translation because of the attention it gives to artistic elements in the Scriptures, while remaining true to the original language.

4. Not the real name of the publisher or product line.

5. The wisdom from above is meant to free us from the bondage of self-focus. In his cunning way, Satan twists the truth, causing some to fall into the bondage of self-deprecation—especially when we are being abused. If you think you may be in an abusive relationship, please seek the input of a trusted pastor, friend, or therapist before making drastic choices in an attempt to apply the "me-free" message in James 3:14–15 and throughout this book.

6. C. S. Lewis, *Mere Christianity* (San Francisco, CA: Harper One, 1952), 122.

7. Lewis, *Mere Christianity*, 122.

8. Timothy Keller, *The Freedom of Self-Forgetfulness* (Chorley, England: 10 Publishing, 2012), 32.

9. "Julie" did not betray anyone by sharing her story. She only shared her own perspective, and she got permission beforehand.

10. Brené Brown, "Listening to Shame: Brené Brown," TED, March 16, 2012, 20:38, https://youtu.be/psN1DORYYV0.

11. Kenneth E. Bailey, *Paul Through Mediterranean Eyes: Cultural Studies in 1 Corinthians* (Downers Grove, IL: InterVarsity, 2011), 341.

12. See John 1:19–24. John often uses "the Jews" to refer to Jesus's opponents.

13. Keep in mind that John knew nothing of the church or the bride of Christ; those teachings would come later (Matt. 16:18). John was sent to

the Jewish people, whereas the church includes every tribe and tongue (Rev. 7:9). If John had been referring to the church, he would not have said his joy was "complete" (John 3:29).

14. Jeff Manion, "Body Works," Ada Bible Church, December 8, 2019, 47:14, https://www.adabible.org/sermons/bodyworks/.

15. First Corinthians 14:26 gives this as the purpose for our gifts: "Let all things be done for building up [the church]."

16. John Dickson, *Humilitas* (Grand Rapids: Zondervan, 2011), 79.

17. The passages in this lesson do talk about spiritual gifts. But the Spirit often also asks us to use an ability, resource, or position to build up the faith of others—which is the goal of spiritual gifts (1 Cor. 14:26).

Chapter Two: Comparing Your Sin and Mine

1. Kenneth E. Bailey, *Through Peasant Eyes: A Literary-Cultural Approach to the Parables of Luke*, combined ed. (Grand Rapids: Eerdmans, 1983), 145.

2. Bailey, *Through Peasant Eyes*, 148.

3. *ESV Study Bible* (Wheaton, IL: Crossway Bibles, 2008), 1793–94.

4. Ed Stetzer, *Christians in the Age of Outrage: How to Bring Our Best When the World Is at Its Worst* (Carol Stream, IL: Tyndale Momentum, 2018), 204–205.

5. Stetzer, *Christians in the Age of Outrage*, 206.

6. Klyne R. Snodgrass, *Stories with Intent: A Comprehensive Guide to the Parables of Jesus*, 2nd ed. (Grand Rapids: Eerdmans, 2018), 467.

7. Timothy Keller, *The Freedom of Self-Forgetfulness* (Chorley, England: 10 Publishing, 2012), 37–38.

8. Milton Vincent, *A Gospel Primer* (Bemidji, MN: Focus, 2011), 34.

9. Vincent, *A Gospel Primer*, 34.

10. Tim Keller, *Paul's Letter to the Galatians* (New York: Redeemer Presbyterian Church, 2003), 2.

11. Jeff Manion, "The Unexpected Guest," Ada Bible Church, June 23, 2019, 45:54 https://www.adabible.org/sermons/the-unexpected-guest/.

12. Snodgrass, *Stories with Intent*, 645.

13. Snodgrass, *Stories with Intent*, 82.

14. *ESV Study Bible*, 1966.

15. John MacArthur, "The Transformed Sinner," Grace to You, April 14, 2002, https://www.gty.org/library/sermons-library/42-101/the-transformed-sinner.

16. Timothy Keller, "The Two Debtors: On Devotion," *Timothy Keller Sermon Archive* (New York: Redeemer Presbyterian Church, 2013), n.p. Accessed through Logos Bible Software.

Chapter Three: Comparing Wealth

1. L. G. Whitlock, R. C. Sproul, B. K. Waltke, and M. Silva, *The Reformation Study Bible: Bringing the Light of the Reformation to Scripture, New King James Version*, (Nashville: Thomas Nelson, 1995), n.p. Accessed through Logos Bible Software on Luke 15:20.

2. Randy Alcorn, *The Treasure Principle: Unlocking the Secret of Joyful Giving* (Sisters, OR: Multnomah, 2001), 77.

3. Listen to more from my friends Bruce and Sue at Generous Giving, https://generousgiving.org/media/videos/bruce-and-sue-osterink -2014-celebration-of-generosity.

4. If you're thinking this story sounds vaguely familiar, I told a similar story in *Control Girl* about a dinner date that ended with slammed doors. That was a year prior to this, and obviously I still had (and have) lots to learn.

5. Tim Keller, "The Gospel, Grace, and Living," Generous Giving, accessed March 6, 2020, 16:00, https://generousgiving.org/media/videos /tim-keller-the-gospel-grace-and-giving.

6. Randy Alcorn, *The Treasure Principle*, 19.

7. Job 1:6–7 tells about Satan coming to present himself to God after walking to and fro on the earth.

8. Randy Alcorn, *Money, Possessions, and Eternity* (Carol Stream, IL: Tyndale, 2003), 125.

Chapter Four: Comparing Skin-Deep Packaging

1. Remember that this is the title I like to give the Sermon on the Mount, since it's the first time Jesus introduced the upside-down kingdom and invited everybody in.

2. Vaneetha Rendall Risner, *The Scars That Have Shaped Me* (Minneapolis, MN: Desiring God, 2016), 7, 20, 25, 46–49.

3. Aaron Buer, "You're Missing It!," Ada Bible Church, July 29, 2019, 47:10, https://vimeo.com/350740625.

4. Cameron Russell, "Looks Aren't Everything. Believe Me, I'm a Model," TED, October 2012, 9:23, https://www.ted.com/talks/cameron_russell _looks_aren_t_everything_believe_me_i_m_a_model.

5. Frederick Dale Bruner, *The Christbook: A Historical/Theological Commentary, Matthew 1–12* (Waco, TX: Word, 1987), 452.

6. Nancy DeMoss Wolgemuth, *Lies Women Believe and the Truth That Sets Them Free* (Chicago: Moody Publishers, 2018), 69.

Chapter Five: Comparing Our Ministries

1. John MacArthur, *Parables: The Mysteries of God's Kingdom Revealed Through the Stories Jesus Told* (Nashville: Thomas Nelson, 2015), 62.

2. Michael Rydelnik and Michael Vanlaningham, eds., *The Moody Bible Commentary*, vol. 1 (Chicago: Moody Publishers, 2014), 1511. See also Jen Wilkin, "4 Ways to Battle Bitterness," The Gospel Coalition, February 2, 2016, https://www.thegospelcoalition.org/article/4-ways-to-battle-bitterness.

3. Kevin DeYoung, "Fairness or Grace?," Truth for Life, May 15, 2013, 51:14, https://www.youtube.com/watch?v=6NLDhb_3NHQ.

4. J. A. Bengel, *Gnomon of the New Testament* (New York: Sheldon and Co., 1862), 240.

5. Steve Bezner, "On Being Matt Chandler's Roommate," For the Church, November 20, 2015, https://ftc.co/resource-library/blog-entries/on-being-matt-chandlers-roommate.

Chapter Six: Comparing Status

1. Linda Hirshman, "Unleashing the Wrath of Stay-at-Home Moms," *Washington Post*, June 18, 2006, http://www.washingtonpost.com/wp-dyn/content/article/2006/06/16/AR2006061601766.html.

2. John Dickson, *Humilitas* (Grand Rapids: Zondervan, 2011), 29.

3. Frederick Dale Bruner, *Matthew: A Commentary, Volume 2: The Churchbook, Matthew 13–28,* rev. ed. (Grand Rapids: Eerdmans, 2004), 211.

4. See Linda Barrick, *Miracle for Jen* (Carol Stream, IL: Tyndale, 2013).

5. *ESV Study Bible* (Wheaton, IL: Crossway Bibles, 2008), 1863.

6. Matthew Henry, *Matthew Henry's Commentary on the Whole Bible* (Peabody, MA: Hendrickson, 1991), 289.

7. This is an estimate, which places Jesus's resurrection around AD 30, then accounts for Paul's description in Galatians 2:1 of a fourteen-year gap that coincides with Acts 11:30, as well as Acts 12:1, which opens with, "About that time . . ."

8. This lesson is based largely on my article "Broken and Poured Out," which appeared on the *True Woman* blog on May 3, 2018, https://www.reviveourhearts.com/true-woman/blog/broken-and-poured-out/. Rights owned by the author.